THE YALE SHAKESPEARE

EDITED BY

WILBUR L. CROSS   **TUCKER BROOKE**

PUBLISHED UNDER THE DIRECTION
OF THE
DEPARTMENT OF ENGLISH, YALE UNIVERSITY,
ON THE FUND
GIVEN TO THE YALE UNIVERSITY PRESS IN 1917
BY THE MEMBERS OF THE
KINGSLEY TRUST ASSOCIATION
(SCROLL AND KEY SOCIETY OF YALE COLLEGE)
TO COMMEMORATE THE SEVENTY-FIFTH ANNIVERSARY
OF THE FOUNDING OF THE SOCIETY

·: *The Yale Shakespeare* :·

SHAKESPEARE'S SONNETS

EDITED BY

EDWARD BLISS REED

NEW HAVEN AND LONDON · YALE UNIVERSITY PRESS

CONTENTS

		PAGE
THE TEXT	. . . . . .	1
NOTES	. . . . . .	78
APPENDIX A.	History of the Sonnets . .	91
APPENDIX B.	Problems of the Sonnets . .	93
APPENDIX C.	The Sonnet and Elizabethan Sonneteers . . .	95
APPENDIX D.	The Text of the Present Edition	97
APPENDIX E.	Suggestions for Collateral Reading	98
INDEX OF WORDS GLOSSED	. . . .	100

The facsimile opposite represents the title-page of the Elizabethan Club copy of the first quarto (1609).

SHAKE-SPEARES

SONNETS

Neuer before Imprinted.

AT LONDON
By *G. Eld* for *T. T.* and are
to be folde by *Iohn Wright,* dwelling
at Chrift Church gate.
1609.

TO · THE · ONLIE · BEGETTER · OF ·
THESE · INSUING · SONNETS ·
MR. W. H. ALL · HAPPINESSE ·
AND · THAT · ETERNITIE ·   4
PROMISED ·
BY ·
OUR · EVER-LIVING · POET ·
WISHETH ·   8
THE · WELL-WISHING ·
ADVENTURER · IN ·
SETTING ·
FORTH ·   12

T. T.

1 Onlie begetter: *only inspirer (?)*; *cf. n.*   3 Mr. W. H.; *cf. n.*
10-12 Adventurer in setting forth: *publisher*   13 T. T.; *cf. n.*

Shakespeare's Sonnets

1

From fairest creatures we desire increase,
That thereby beauty's rose might never die,
But as the riper should by time decease,
His tender heir might bear his memory: **4**
But thou, contracted to thine own bright eyes,
Feed'st thy light's flame with self-substantial fuel,
Making a famine where abundance lies,
Thyself thy foe, to thy sweet self too cruel.   **8**
Thou that art now the world's fresh ornament
And only herald to the gaudy spring,
Within thine own bud buriest thy content
And, tender churl, mak'st waste in niggarding.   **12**
   Pity the world, or else this glutton be,
   To eat the world's due, by the grave and thee.

2

When forty winters shall besiege thy brow,
And dig deep trenches in thy beauty's field,
Thy youth's proud livery, so gaz'd on now,
Will be a tatter'd weed, of small worth held: **4**
Then being ask'd where all thy beauty lies,
Where all the treasure of thy lusty days,
To say, within thine own deep-sunken eyes,
Were an all-eating shame and thriftless praise.   **8**
How much more praise deserv'd thy beauty's use,
If thou couldst answer, 'This fair child of mine
Shall sum my count, and make my old excuse,'
Proving his beauty by succession thine!   **12**
   This were to be new made when thou art old,
   And see thy blood warm when thou feel'st it cold.

1-14 *Cf. n.*   5 contracted: *betrothed*
6 Feed'st . . . fuel; *cf. n.*   11 content: *desire; cf. n.*
13, 14 Pity the world . . . and thee; *cf. n.*   3 livery: *dress*
4 weed: *garment*   11 old excuse: *excuse for my old age*

3

Look in thy glass, and tell the face thou viewest
Now is the time that face should form another;
Whose fresh repair if now thou not renewest,
Thou dost beguile the world, unbless some mother,   4
For where is she so fair whose unear'd womb
Disdains the tillage of thy husbandry?
Or who is he so fond will be the tomb
Of his self-love, to stop posterity?   8
Thou art thy mother's glass, and she in thee
Calls back the lovely April of her prime;
So thou through windows of thine age shalt see,
Despite of wrinkles, this thy golden time.   12
    But if thou live, remember'd not to be,
      Die single, and thine image dies with thee.

4

Unthrifty loveliness, why dost thou spend
Upon thyself thy beauty's legacy?
Nature's bequest gives nothing, but doth lend,
And being frank, she lends to those are free: 4
Then, beauteous niggard, why dost thou abuse
The bounteous largess given thee to give?
Profitless usurer, why dost thou use
So great a sum of sums, yet canst not live?   8
For having traffic with thyself alone,
Thou of thyself thy sweet self dost deceive:
Then how, when Nature calls thee to be gone,
What acceptable audit canst thou leave?   12
    Thy unus'd beauty must be tomb'd with thee,
      Which used, lives th' executor to be.

3 fresh repair: *healthful state*   5 unear'd: *untilled*
7 fond: *foolish*
13 remember'd not to be: *not caring to be remembered*
4 frank: *liberal*   free: *generous*

5

Those hours, that with gentle work did frame
The lovely gaze where every eye doth dwell,
Will play the tyrants to the very same
And that unfair which fairly doth excel;　　　4
For never-resting time leads summer on
To hideous winter, and confounds him there;
Sap check'd with frost, and lusty leaves quite gone,
Beauty o'ersnow'd and bareness everywhere:　　　8
Then, were not summer's distillation left,
A liquid prisoner pent in walls of glass,
Beauty's effect with beauty were bereft,
Nor it, nor no remembrance what it was:　　　12
　　But flowers distill'd, though they with winter meet,
　　Leese but their show; their substance still lives
　　　sweet.

6

Then let not winter's ragged hand deface
In thee thy summer, ere thou be distill'd:
Make sweet some vial; treasure thou some place
With beauty's treasure, ere it be self-kill'd.　　　4
That use is not forbidden usury,
Which happies those that pay the willing loan;
That's for thyself to breed another thee,
Or ten times happier, be it ten for one;　　　8
Ten times thyself were happier than thou art,
If ten of thine ten times refigur'd thee;
Then what could death do, if thou shouldst depart,
Leaving thee living in posterity?　　　12
　　Be not self-will'd, for thou art much too fair
　　To be death's conquest and make worms thine heir.

2 gaze: *object of sight, sight*
4 unfair: *deprive of beauty*　　　fairly: *in beauty*
6 confounds: *destroys*　　　9, 10 *Cf. n.*　　　12 it: *would it remain*
14 Leese: *lose*　　　1 ragged: *rugged*　　　3 treasure: *enrich*
5 use: *interest*　　　6 happies: *makes happy*
10 refigur'd: *reproduced in appearance*

7

Lo, in the orient when the gracious light
Lifts up his burning head, each under eye
Doth homage to his new-appearing sight,
Serving with looks his sacred majesty;   4
And having climb'd the steep-up heavenly hill,
Resembling strong youth in his middle age,
Yet mortal looks adore his beauty still,
Attending on his golden pilgrimage;   8
But when from highmost pitch, with weary car,
Like feeble age, he reeleth from the day,
The eyes, 'fore duteous, now converted are
From his low tract, and look another way: 12
    So thou, thyself outgoing in thy noon,
    Unlook'd on diest, unless thou get a son.

8

Music to hear, why hear'st thou music sadly?
Sweets with sweets war not, joy delights in joy:
Why lov'st thou that which thou receiv'st not gladly,
Or else receiv'st with pleasure thine annoy?   4
If the true concord of well-tuned sounds,
By unions married, do offend thine ear,
They do but sweetly chide thee, who confounds
In singleness the parts that thou shouldst bear.   8
Mark how one string, sweet husband to another,
Strikes each in each by mutual ordering;
Resembling sire and child and happy mother,
Who, all in one, one pleasing note do sing: 12
    Whose speechless song, being many, seeming one,
    Sings this to thee: 'Thou single wilt prove none.'

9-12 *Cf. n.*   9 highmost pitch: *highest elevation*
11 converted: *turned away*   12 tract: *course*
13 thyself outgoing . . . noon: *passing beyond your noon of beauty*
1 Music to hear: *you whose voice is music*
10 mutual ordering: *ordered harmony*
14 'Thou single wilt prove none'; *cf. n.*

9

Is it for fear to wet a widow's eye
That thou consum'st thyself in single life?
Ah! if thou issueless shalt hap to die,
The world will wail thee, like a makeless wife;   4
The world will be thy widow, and still weep
That thou no form of thee hast left behind,
When every private widow well may keep
By children's eyes her husband's shape in mind.   8
Look, what an unthrift in the world doth spend
Shifts but his place, for still the world enjoys it;
But beauty's waste hath in the world an end,
And kept unus'd, the user so destroys it.   12
  No love toward others in that bosom sits
  That on himself such murderous shame commits.

10

For shame deny that thou bear'st love to any,
Who for thyself art so unprovident.
Grant, if thou wilt, thou art belov'd of many,
But that thou none lov'st is most evident;   4
For thou art so possess'd with murderous hate
That 'gainst thyself thou stick'st not to conspire,
Seeking that beauteous roof to ruinate
Which to repair should be thy chief desire.   8
O, change thy thought, that I may change my mind:
Shall hate be fairer lodg'd than gentle love?
Be, as thy presence is, gracious and kind,
Or to thyself at least kind-hearted prove: 12
  Make thee another self, for love of me,
  That beauty still may live in thine or thee.

4 makeless: *mateless*   5 still: *continually*
10 his: *its*   7 beauteous roof: *your body*

11

As fast as thou shalt wane, so fast thou grow'st
In one of thine, from that which thou departest;
And that fresh blood which youngly thou bestow'st
Thou mayst call thine when thou from youth con-
　　　　vertest.　　　　　　　　　　　　　　　　　4
Herein lies wisdom, beauty and increase;
Without this, folly, age and cold decay:
If all were minded so, the times should cease
And threescore year would make the world away.　　8
Let those whom Nature hath not made for store,
Harsh, featureless and rude, barrenly perish:
Look, whom she best endow'd she gave the more;
Which bounteous gift thou shouldst in bounty cherish:
　　She carv'd thee for her seal, and meant thereby　13
　　Thou shouldst print more, nor let that copy die.

12

When I do count the clock that tells the time,
And see the brave day sunk in hideous night;
When I behold the violet past prime,
And sable curls, all silver'd o'er with white;　　　4
When lofty trees I see barren of leaves,
Which erst from heat did canopy the herd,
And summer's green all girded up in sheaves,
Borne on the bier with white and bristly beard,　　8
Then of thy beauty do I question make,
That thou among the wastes of time must go,
Since sweets and beauties do themselves forsake
And die as fast as they see others grow;　　　　12
　　And nothing 'gainst Time's scythe can make defence
　　Save breed, to brave him when he takes thee hence.

2 departest: *takest leave of*
3 youngly: *in youth*　　　bestow'st: *layest out, spendest*
4 convertest: *changest*
11 Look, . . . the more; *cf. n.*
6 erst: *formerly*
9 for store: *for breeding*
2 brave: *beautiful*
9 question make: *meditate*

13

O that you were yourself ! but, love, you are
No longer yours than you yourself here live:
Against this coming end you should prepare,
And your sweet semblance to some other give: 4
So should that beauty which you hold in lease
Find no determination; then you were
Yourself again, after yourself's decease,
When your sweet issue your sweet form should bear. 8
Who lets so fair a house fall to decay,
Which husbandry in honour might uphold
Against the stormy gusts of winter's day
And barren rage of death's eternal cold?   12
   O, none but unthrifts. Dear my love, you know
   You had a father: let your son say so.

14

Not from the stars do I my judgment pluck;
And yet methinks I have astronomy,
But not to tell of good or evil luck,
Of plagues, of dearths, or seasons' quality;   4
Nor can I fortune to brief minutes tell,
Pointing to each his thunder, rain, and wind,
Or say with princes if it shall go well,
By oft predict that I in heaven find: 8
But from thine eyes my knowledge I derive,
And, constant stars, in them I read such art
As 'Truth and beauty shall together thrive,
If from thyself to store thou wouldst convert;'   12
   Or else of thee this I prognosticate:
   'Thy end is truth's and beauty's doom and date.'

1 yourself; *cf. n.*   6 determination: *end*   10 husbandry: *thrift*
13 unthrifts: *wastrels*   2 have astronomy: *know astrology*
5 tell: *allot*   6 Pointing: *appointing*
8 oft predict: *frequent predictions*   10 art: *knowledge*
12 If from thyself . . . convert; *cf. n.*   14 date: *end*

15

When I consider everything that grows
Holds in perfection but a little moment,
That this huge stage presenteth nought but shows
Whereon the stars in secret influence comment;   4
When I perceive that men as plants increase,
Cheered and check'd e'en by the self-same sky,
Vaunt in their youthful sap, at height decrease,
And wear their brave state out of memory;   8
Then the conceit of this inconstant stay
Sets you most rich in youth before my sight,
Where wasteful Time debateth with Decay,
To change your day of youth to sullied night;   12
   And, all in war with Time for love of you,
   As he takes from you, I engraft you new.

16

But wherefore do not you a mightier way
Make war upon this bloody tyrant, Time?
And fortify yourself in your decay
With means more blessed than my barren rime?   4
Now stand you on the top of happy hours,
And many maiden gardens, yet unset,
With virtuous wish would bear you living flowers
Much liker than your painted counterfeit: 8
So should the lines of life that life repair,
Which this Time's pencil, or my pupil pen,
Neither in inward worth nor outward fair,
Can make you live yourself in eyes of men.   12
   To give away yourself, keeps yourself still;
   And you must live, drawn by your own sweet skill.

4 influence; *cf. n.*   6 Cheered and check'd: *encouraged and repressed*
7 Vaunt: *exult*   at height: *when fully developed*
8 And wear . . . memory: *and outlast the memory of their prime*
9 conceit: *thought*   inconstant stay: *transitory state of being*
11 debateth: *takes counsel with*
14 engraft you new: *renew your beauty (by my verse)*
6 unset: *not planted*   8 painted counterfeit: *portrait*
9 lines of life: *children*   10 Which this . . . pupil pen; *cf. n.*
11 fair: *beauty*   13 To give away yourself: *to beget children*

17

Who will believe my verse in time to come,
If it were fill'd with your most high deserts?
Though yet, heaven knows, it is but as a tomb
Which hides your life and shows not half your parts. 4
If I could write the beauty of your eyes
And in fresh numbers number all your graces,
The age to come would say, 'This poet lies;
Such heavenly touches ne'er touch'd earthly faces.' 8
So should my papers, yellow'd with their age,
Be scorn'd, like old men of less truth than tongue,
And your true rights be term'd a poet's rage
And stretched metre of an antique song: 12
  But were some child of yours alive that time,
  You should live twice,—in it and in my rime.

18

Shall I compare thee to a summer's day?
Thou art more lovely and more temperate:
Rough winds do shake the darling buds of May,
And summer's lease hath all too short a date: 4
Sometime too hot the eye of heaven shines,
And often is his gold complexion dimm'd;
And every fair from fair sometime declines,
By chance, or nature's changing course untrimm'd; 8
But thy eternal summer shall not fade,
Nor lose possession of that fair thou ow'st,
Nor shall death brag thou wander'st in his shade,
When in eternal lines to time thou grow'st; 12
  So long as man can breathe, or eyes can see,
  So long lives this, and this gives life to thee.

11 rage: *enthusiasm*   12 stretched: *strained, exaggerated*
1-14 *Cf. n.*   8 untrimm'd: *deprived of adornment*
10 ow'st: *ownest*

19

Devouring Time, blunt thou the lion's paws,
And make the earth devour her own sweet brood;
Pluck the keen teeth from the fierce tiger's jaws,
And burn the long-liv'd phœnix in her blood;   4
Make glad and sorry seasons as thou fleets,
And do whate'er thou wilt, swift-footed Time,
To the wide world and all her fading sweets;
But I forbid thee one most heinous crime: 8
O, carve not with thy hours my love's fair brow,
Nor draw no lines there with thine antique pen;
Him in thy course untainted do allow
For beauty's pattern to succeeding men.   12
     Yet do thy worst, old Time: despite thy wrong,
     My love shall in my verse ever live young.

20

A woman's face with Nature's own hand painted
Hast thou, the master-mistress of my passion;
A woman's gentle heart, but not acquainted
With shifting change, as is false women's fashion;   4]
An eye more bright than theirs, less false in rolling,
Gilding the object whereupon it gazeth;
A man in hue all hues in his controlling,
Which steals men's eyes and women's souls amazeth.   8]
And for a woman wert thou first created;
Till Nature, as she wrought thee, fell a-doting,
And by addition me of thee defeated,
By adding one thing to my purpose nothing.   12]
     But since she prick'd thee out for women's pleasure,
     Mine be thy love, and thy love's use their treasure.

---

5 fleets: *hastest*   10 antique; *cf. n.*   1–14 *Cf. n.*
7 A man in hue . . . controlling; *cf. n.*   11 defeated: *deprived*

21

So is it not with me as with that Muse
Stirr'd by a painted beauty to his verse,
Who heaven itself for ornament doth use
And every fair with his fair doth rehearse,   4
Making a couplement of proud compare,
With sun and moon, with earth and sea's rich gems,
With April's first-born flowers, and all things rare
That heaven's air in this huge rondure hems.   8
O let me, true in love, but truly write,
And then believe me, my love is as fair
As any mother's child, though not so bright
As those gold candles fix'd in heaven's air: 12
    Let them say more that like of hear-say well;
    I will not praise that purpose not to sell.

22

My glass shall not persuade me I am old,
So long as youth and thou are of one date;
But when in thee time's furrows I behold,
Then look I death my days should expiate.   4
For all that beauty that doth cover thee
Is but the seemly raiment of my heart,
Which in thy breast doth live, as thine in me:
How can I then be elder than thou art?   8
O therefore, love, be of thyself so wary
As I, not for myself, but for thee will;
Bearing thy heart, which I will keep so chary
As tender nurse her babe from faring ill.   12
    Presume not on thy heart when mine is slain;
    Thou gav'st me thine, not to give back again.

1 Muse: *poet*   4 rehearse: *relate*
5 Making . . . compare: *joining in proud comparison*
8 rondure: *circle*   4 expiate: *end*
13 Presume not on: *think not to regain*

23

As an unperfect actor on the stage,
Who with his fear is put besides his part,
Or some fierce thing replete with too much rage,
Whose strength's abundance weakens his own heart; 4
So I, for fear of trust, forget to say
The perfect ceremony of love's rite,
And in mine own love's strength seem to decay,
O'ercharg'd with burden of mine own love's might. 8
O, let my books be then the eloquence
And dumb presagers of my speaking breast,
Who plead for love, and look for recompense,
More than that tongue that more hath more express'd.
   O, learn to read what silent love hath writ: 13
   To hear with eyes belongs to love's fine wit.

24

Mine eye hath play'd the painter and hath stell'd
Thy beauty's form in table of my heart;
My body is the frame wherein 'tis held,
And perspective it is best painter's art. 4
For through the painter must you see his skill,
To find where your true image pictur'd lies,
Which in my bosom's shop is hanging still,
That hath his windows glazed with thine eyes. 8
Now see what good turns eyes for eyes have done:
Mine eyes have drawn thy shape, and thine for me
Are windows to my breast, where-through the sun
Delights to peep, to gaze therein on thee; 12
   Yet eyes this cunning want to grace their art,
   They draw but what they see, know not the heart.

2 put besides: *put out of*
5 fear of trust: *fearing to trust myself* (?), *lacking all self-confidence* (?)   10 presagers: *indicators*
12 that more . . . express'd: *that more eloquently has told of greater devotion*   1 stell'd: *placed, engraved* (?)
2 table: *surface on which picture is drawn*   4 perspective; *cf. n.*

25

Let those who are in favour with their stars
Of public honour and proud titles boast,
Whilst I, whom fortune of such triumph bars,
Unlook'd for joy in that I honour most.   4
Great princes' favourites their fair leaves spread
But as the marigold at the sun's eye,
And in themselves their pride lies buried,
For at a frown they in their glory die.   8
The painful warrior famoused for fight,
After a thousand victories once foil'd,
Is from the book of honour razed quite,
And all the rest forgot for which he toil'd: 12
    Then happy I, that love and am belov'd,
    Where I may not remove nor be remov'd.

26

Lord of my love, to whom in vassalage
Thy merit hath my duty strongly knit,
To thee I send this written ambassage,
To witness duty, not to show my wit: 4
Duty so great, which wit so poor as mine
May make seem bare, in wanting words to show it,
But that I hope some good conceit of thine
In thy soul's thought, all naked, will bestow it;   8
Till whatsoever star that guides my moving
Points on me graciously with fair aspect,
And puts apparel on my tatter'd loving,
To show me worthy of thy sweet respect: 12
    Then may I dare to boast how I do love thee;
    Till then, not show my head where thou mayst prove
    me.

4 Unlook'd for: *unexpectedly*   6 But: *only*
7 And in . . . buried: *their pride soon perishes with them*
1-14 *Cf. n.*   3 ambassage: *message*   10 Points: *shines*

27

Weary with toil, I haste me to my bed,
The dear repose for limbs with travel tir'd;
But then begins a journey in my head
To work my mind, when body's work's expir'd: 4
For then my thoughts—from far where I abide—
Intend a zealous pilgrimage to thee,
And keep my drooping eyelids open wide,
Looking on darkness which the blind do see: 8
Save that my soul's imaginary sight
Presents thy shadow to my sightless view,
Which, like a jewel hung in ghastly night,
Makes black night beauteous and her old face new.   12
    Lo! thus, by day my limbs, by night my mind,
      For thee, and for myself, no quiet find.

28

How can I then return in happy plight,
That am debarr'd the benefit of rest?
When day's oppression is not eas'd by night,
But day by night, and night by day oppress'd,   4
And each, though enemies to either's reign,
Do in consent shake hands to torture me,
The one by toil, the other to complain
How far I toil, still further off from thee.   8
I tell the day, to please him, thou art bright
And dost him grace when clouds do blot the heaven:
So flatter I the swart-complexion'd night,
When sparkling stars twire not thou gild'st the even. 12
    But day doth daily draw my sorrows longer,
      And night doth nightly make grief's strength seem
      stronger.

5 Intend: *plan, set about*   9 imaginary: *imaginative*
6 shake hands: *conspire*   12 twire: *peep, twinkle*

29

When, in disgrace with fortune and men's eyes,
I all alone beweep my outcast state,
And trouble deaf heaven with my bootless cries,
And look upon myself, and curse my fate,   4
Wishing me like to one more rich in hope,
Featur'd like him, like him with friends possess'd,
Desiring this man's art, and that man's scope,
With what I most enjoy contented least;   8
Yet in these thoughts myself almost despising,
Haply I think on thee,—and then my state,
Like to the lark at break of day arising
From sullen earth, sings hymns at heaven's gate;   12
 For thy sweet love remember'd such wealth brings
 That then I scorn to change my state with kings.

30

When to the sessions of sweet silent thought
I summon up remembrance of things past,
I sigh the lack of many a thing I sought,
And with old woes new wail my dear times' waste: 4
Then can I drown an eye, unus'd to flow,
For precious friends hid in death's dateless night,
And weep afresh love's long since cancell'd woe,
And moan the expense of many a vanish'd sight: 8
Then can I grieve at grievances foregone,
And heavily from woe to woe tell o'er
The sad account of fore-bemoaned moan,
Which I new pay as if not paid before.   12
 But if the while I think on thee, dear friend,
 All losses are restor'd and sorrows end.

7 scope: *range of opportunity*   1 sessions: *sittings of court*
4 new wail: *bewail anew*   6 dateless: *endless*
8 expense: *loss*   9 grievances foregone: *former griefs*
10 tell: *count*

31

Thy bosom is endeared with all hearts
Which I by lacking have supposed dead;
And there reigns Love, and all Love's loving parts,
And all those friends which I thought buried.　　　　4
How many a holy and obsequious tear
Hath dear religious love stol'n from mine eye,
As interest of the dead, which now appear
But things remov'd that hidden in thee lie!　　　　8
Thou art the grave where buried love doth live,
Hung with the trophies of my lovers gone,
Who all their parts of me to thee did give,
That due of many now is thine alone:　　　　12
　　Their images I lov'd I view in thee,
　　And thou—all they—hast all the all of me.

32

If thou survive my well-contented day,
When that churl Death my bones with dust shall cover,
And shalt by fortune once more re-survey
These poor rude lines of thy deceased lover,　　　　4
Compare them with the bettering of the time,
And though they be outstripp'd by every pen,
Reserve them for my love, not for their rime,
Exceeded by the height of happier men.　　　　8
O, then vouchsafe me but this loving thought:
'Had my friend's Muse grown with this growing age,
A dearer birth than this his love had brought,
To march in ranks of better equipage:　　　　12
　　But since he died, and poets better prove,
　　Theirs for their style I'll read, his for his love.'

1 endeared: *made precious*　　　　5 obsequious: *dutiful, regardful*
6 religious: *devoted*　　　　7 interest: *the right, the due*
11 parts of me: *claims in me*
12 That . . . many: *so that which many once deserved*
13 Their . . . lov'd: *the images of those I loved*
1 my well-contented day: *the day I shall be well contented with*
5 bettering . . . time: *better works of later time*
7 Reserve: *retain*　　　　12 better equipage: *richer equipment*

33

Full many a glorious morning have I seen
Flatter the mountain-tops with sovereign eye,
Kissing with golden face the meadows green,
Gilding pale streams with heavenly alchemy;   4
Anon permit the basest clouds to ride
With ugly rack on his celestial face,
And from the forlorn world his visage hide,
Stealing unseen to west with this disgrace: 8
Even so my sun one early morn did shine,
With all-triumphant splendour on my brow;
But, out! alack! he was but one hour mine,
The region cloud hath mask'd him from me now.   12
   Yet him for this my love no whit disdaineth;
   Suns of the world may stain when heaven's sun
     staineth.

34

Why didst thou promise such a beauteous day,
And make me travel forth without my cloak,
To let base clouds o'ertake me in my way,
Hiding thy bravery in their rotten smoke?   4
'Tis not enough that through the cloud thou break,
To dry the rain on my storm-beaten face,
For no man well of such a salve can speak
That heals the wound and cures not the disgrace: 8
Nor can thy shame give physic to my grief;
Though thou repent, yet I have still the loss:
The offender's sorrow lends but weak relief
To him that bears the strong offence's cross.   12
   Ah! but those tears are pearl which thy love sheds,
   And they are rich and ransom all ill deeds.

2 sovereign eye: *eye of a king*   6 rack: *clouds in the upper air*
8 disgrace: *disfigurement*   12 region cloud: *cloud of heaven*
14 may stain: *may be obscured*   staineth: *is obscured*
4 bravery: *splendor*   rotten smoke: *unwholesome mist*
13, 14 Ah! but those tears . . . ill deeds; *cf. n.*

35

No more be griev'd at that which thou hast done:
Roses have thorns, and silver fountains mud;
Clouds and eclipses stain both moon and sun,
And loathsome canker lives in sweetest bud.   4
All men make faults, and even I in this,
Authorising thy trespass with compare,
Myself corrupting, salving thy amiss,
Excusing thy sins more than thy sins are;   8
For to thy sensual fault I bring in sense,—
Thy adverse party is thy advocate,—
And 'gainst myself a lawful plea commence:
Such civil war is in my love and hate,   12
    That I an accessary needs must be
    To that sweet thief which sourly robs from me.

36

Let me confess that we two must be twain,
Although our undivided loves are one:
So shall those blots that do with me remain,
Without thy help, by me be borne alone.   4
In our two loves there is but one respect,
Though in our lives a separable spite,
Which, though it alter not love's sole effect,
Yet doth it steal sweet hours from love's delight.   8
I may not evermore acknowledge thee,
Lest my bewailed guilt should do thee shame,
Nor thou with public kindness honour me,
Unless thou take that honour from thy name: 12
    But do not so; I love thee in such sort
    As thou being mine, mine is thy good report.

2 fountains: *springs*   3 stain: *dim*
6 Authorising: *sanctioning*   with compare: *by these comparisons*
7 amiss: *fauit*   8 Excusing thy sins; *cf. n.*   9 sense; *cf. n.*
13 accessary: *accessory, helper*   14 sourly: *cruelly*
5 respect: *consideration, regard*   6 separable: *dividing, separating*
13, 14 But do not so . . . good report; *cf. n.*

37

As a decrepit father takes delight
To see his active child do deeds of youth,
So I, made lame by fortune's dearest spite,
Take all my comfort of thy worth and truth;   4
For whether beauty, birth, or wealth, or wit,
Or any of these all, or all, or more,
Entitled in thy parts do crowned sit,
I make my love engrafted to this store: 8
So then I am not lame, poor, nor despis'd,
Whilst that this shadow doth such substance give
That I in thy abundance am suffic'd
And by a part of all thy glory live.   12
   Look what is best, that best I wish in thee:
   This wish I have; then ten times happy me!

38

How can my Muse want subject to invent,
While thou dost breathe, that pour'st into my verse
Thine own sweet argument, too excellent
For every vulgar paper to rehearse?   4
O, give thyself the thanks, if aught in me
Worthy perusal stand against thy sight;
For who's so dumb that cannot write to thee,
When thou thyself dost give invention light?   8
Be thou the tenth Muse, ten times more in worth
Than those old nine which rimers invoke;
And he that calls on thee, let him bring forth
Eternal numbers to outlive long date.   12
   If my slight Muse do please these curious days,
   The pain be mine, but thine shall be the praise.

3 dearest spite: *worst malice*   5-7 *Cf. n.*   7 Entitled: *rightfully*
8 engrafted: *added to*   10 shadow: *imagination*
11 suffic'd: *contented*   3 argument: *theme*   4 rehearse: *narrate*
6 against: *in*   8 invention: *creative imagination*
13 curious: *fastidious*   14 pain: *labour*

39

O, how thy worth with manners may I sing,
When thou art all the better part of me?
What can mine own praise to mine own self bring?
And what is 't but mine own when I praise thee?   4
Even for this let us divided live,
And our dear love lose name of single one,
That by this separation I may give
That due to thee, which thou deserv'st alone.   8
O absence! what a torment wouldst thou prove,
Were it not thy sour leisure gave sweet leave
To entertain the time with thoughts of love,
Which time and thoughts so sweetly doth deceive,   12
     And that thou teachest how to make one twain,
     By praising him here who doth hence remain.

40

Take all my loves, my love, yea, take them all;
What hast thou then more than thou hadst before?
No love, my love, that thou mayst true love call;
All mine was thine before thou hadst this more.   4
Then, if for my love thou my love receivest,
I cannot blame thee for my love thou usest;
But yet be blam'd, if thou thyself deceivest
By wilful taste of what thyself refusest.   8
I do forgive thy robbery, gentle thief,
Although thou steal thee all my poverty;
And yet, love knows it is a greater grief
To bear love's wrong than hate's known injury.   12
     Lascivious grace, in whom all ill well shows,
     Kill me with spites; yet we must not be foes.

---

1 with manners: *becomingly*
13, 14 And that thou teachest . . . remain; *cf. n.*
5 if for: *if because of (?), if instead of (?)
receivest the woman I love*
8 By wilful taste . . . refusest; *cf. n.*

11 entertain: *pass away*
1-14 *Cf. n.*
my love receivest:
6 for: *because*
14 spites: *injuries*

41

Those pretty wrongs that liberty commits,
When I am sometimes absent from thy heart,
Thy beauty and thy years full well befits,
For still temptation follows where thou art.   **4**
Gentle thou art, and therefore to be won,
Beauteous thou art, therefore to be assail'd;
And when a woman woos, what woman's son
Will sourly leave her till she have prevail'd?   **8**
Ay me! but yet thou mightst my seat forbear,
And chide thy beauty and thy straying youth,
Who lead thee in their riot even there
Where thou art forc'd to break a twofold truth;—   **12**
    Hers, by thy beauty tempting her to thee,
    Thine, by thy beauty being false to me.

42

That thou hast her, it is not all my grief,
And yet it may be said I lov'd her dearly;
That she hath thee, is of my wailing chief,
A loss in love that touches me more nearly.   **4**
Loving offenders, thus I will excuse ye:
Thou dost love her, because thou know'st I love her;
And for my sake even so doth she abuse me,
Suffering my friend for my sake to approve her.   **8**
If I lose thee, my loss is my love's gain,
And losing her, my friend hath found that loss;
Both find each other, and I lose both twain,
And both for my sake lay on me this cross: **12**
    But here's the joy; my friend and I are one;
    Sweet flattery! then she loves but me alone.

1 liberty: *license*   3 chief: *the main cause*
7 abuse: *misuse*   8 approve: *like, make trial of* (?)
11 both twain: *both the two*

43

When most I wink, then do mine eyes best see,
For all the day they view things unrespected;
But when I sleep, in dreams they look on thee,
And darkly bright, are bright in dark directed.   4
Then thou, whose shadow shadows doth make bright,
How would thy shadow's form form happy show
To the clear day with thy much clearer light,
When to unseeing eyes thy shade shines so!   8
How would, I say, mine eyes be blessed made
By looking on thee in the living day,
When in dead night thy fair imperfect shade
Through heavy sleep on sightless eyes doth stay!   12
    All days are nights to see till I see thee,
      And nights bright days when dreams do show thee
      me.

44

If the dull substance of my flesh were thought,
Injurious distance should not stop my way;
For then, despite of space, I would be brought,
From limits far remote, where thou dost stay.   4
No matter then although my foot did stand
Upon the furthest earth remov'd from thee;
For nimble thought can jump both sea and land,
As soon as think the place where he would be.   8
But, ah! thought kills me that I am not thought,
To leap large lengths of miles when thou art gone,
But that, so much of earth and water wrought,
I must attend time's leisure with my moan;   12
    Receiving nought by elements so slow
    But heavy tears, badges of either's woe.

1 wink: *close my eyes*   2 unrespected: *unworthy of notice*
4 darkly: *in the dark*
5 whose shadow . . . bright: *whose remembered image makes darkness bright*
6 furthest earth remov'd: *plot of earth most remote*   4 where: *to the place where*
9 thought kills me: *melancholy kills me* (?), *it kills me to think* (?)
11 wrought: *made, created*   14 badges of either's woe; *cf. n.*

45

The other two, slight air and purging fire,
Are both with thee, wherever I abide;
The first my thought, the other my desire,
These present-absent with swift motion slide. 4
For when these quicker elements are gone
In tender embassy of love to thee,
My life, being made of four, with two alone
Sinks down to death, oppress'd with melancholy; 8
Until life's composition be recur'd
By those sweet messengers return'd from thee,
Who even but now come back again, assur'd
Of thy fair health, recounting it to me: 12
    This told, I joy; but then no longer glad,
    I send them back again, and straight grow sad.

46

Mine eye and heart are at a mortal war,
How to divide the conquest of thy sight;
Mine eye my heart thy picture's sight would **bar**,
My heart mine eye the freedom of that right. 4
My heart doth plead that thou in him dost lie,—
A closet never pierc'd with crystal eyes,—
But the defendant doth that plea deny,
And says in him thy fair appearance lies. 8
To 'cide this title is impanelled
A quest of thoughts, all tenants to the heart;
And by their verdict is determined
The clear eye's moiety and the dear heart's part: 12
    As thus; mine eye's due is thine outward part,
    And my heart's right thine inward love of heart.

9 life's composition: *union of the four elements*   recur'd: *restored*
9 impanelled: *enrolled*   10 quest: *jury*   12 moiety: *share*

47

Betwixt mine eye and heart a league is took,
And each doth good turns now unto the other:
When that mine eye is famish'd for a look,
Or heart in love with sighs himself doth smother,   4
With my love's picture then my eye doth feast,
And to the painted banquet bids my heart;
Another time mine eye is my heart's guest,
And in his thoughts of love doth share a part: 8
So, either by thy picture or my love,
Thyself away art present still with me;
For thou not further than my thoughts canst move,
And I am still with them and they with thee;   12
   Or, if they sleep, thy picture in my sight
   Awakes my heart to heart's and eye's delight.

48

How careful was I when I took my way,
Each trifle under truest bars to thrust,
That to my use it might unused stay
From hands of falsehood, in sure wards of trust!   4
But thou, to whom my jewels trifles are,
Most worthy comfort, now my greatest grief,
Thou best of dearest and mine only care,
Art left the prey of every vulgar thief.   8
Thee have I not lock'd up in any chest,
Save where thou art not, though I feel thou art,
Within the gentle closure of my breast,
From whence at pleasure thou mayst come and part;
   And even thence thou wilt be stol'n, I fear,   13
   For truth proves thievish for a prize so dear.

4 himself: *itself*   4 wards of trust: *place of security*
11 closure: *enclosure, confine*

49

Against that time, if ever that time come,
When I shall see thee frown on my defects,
When as thy love hath cast his utmost sum,
Call'd to that audit by advis'd respects;   4
Against that time when thou shalt strangely pass,
And scarcely greet me with that sun, thine eye,
When love, converted from the thing it was,
Shall reasons find of settled gravity;   8
Against that time do I ensconce me here
Within the knowledge of mine own desert,
And this my hand against myself uprear,
To guard the lawful reasons on thy part: 12
   To leave poor me thou hast the strength of laws,
   Since why to love I can allege no cause.

50

How heavy do I journey on the way,
When what I seek, my weary travel's end,
Doth teach that ease and that repose to say,
'Thus far the miles are measur'd from thy friend!'   4
The beast that bears me, tired with my woe,
Plods dully on, to bear that weight in me,
As if by some instinct the wretch did know
His rider lov'd not speed, being made from thee: 8
The bloody spur cannot provoke him on
That sometimes anger thrusts into his hide,
Which heavily he answers with a groan
More sharp to me than spurring to his side;   12
   For that same groan doth put this in my mind:
   My grief lies onward, and my joy behind.

1 Against: *in expectation of*
3 When as: *when*   cast his utmost sum: *added every item*
4 advis'd respects: *careful considerations*   5 strangely: *like a stranger*
8 of settled gravity: *for a grave demeanor*
11 uprear: *raise (as a witness taking the oath)*
8 being made: *if directed*

51

Thus can my love excuse the slow offence
Of my dull bearer when from thee I speed:
From where thou art why should I haste me thence?
Till I return, of posting is no need.   4
O, what excuse will my poor beast then find,
When swift extremity can seem but slow?
Then should I spur, though mounted on the wind,
In winged speed no motion shall I know: 8
Then can no horse with my desire keep pace;
Therefore desire, of perfect'st love being made,
Shall neigh—no dull flesh—in his fiery race;
But love, for love, thus shall excuse my jade,—   12
 'Since from thee going he went wilful-slow,
 Towards thee I'll run and give him leave to go.'

52

So am I as the rich, whose blessed key
Can bring him to his sweet up-locked treasure
The which he will not every hour survey,
For blunting the fine point of seldom pleasure.   4
Therefore are feasts so solemn and so rare,
Since, seldom coming, in the long year set,
Like stones of worth they thinly placed are,
Or captain jewels in the carcanet.   8
So is the time that keeps you as my chest,
Or as the wardrobe which the robe doth hide,
To make some special instant special blest
By new unfolding his imprison'd pride.   12
 Blessed are you, whose worthiness gives scope,
 Being had, to triumph; being lack'd, to hope.

---

1 slow offence: *blameworthy slowness* 6 swift extremity: *extreme speed*
8 In winged speed . . . know: *though moving with the speed of wings,
 I shall not seem to myself to be moving at all*
11 Shall neigh . . . fiery race; *cf. n.*
12 for love: *for the sake of his love* (*shown by the slow gait*)
14 go: *walk*   4 For: *for fear of* seldom: *rarely enjoyed*
5 solemn: *ceremonious*   7 thinly: *widely separated*
8 captain: *chief* carcanet: *necklace* 9 chest: *treasure chest*
12 his . . . pride: *its gorgeous contents* 13 scope: *opportunity*

53

What is your substance, whereof are you made,
That millions of strange shadows on you tend?
Since every one hath, every one, one shade,
And you, but one, can every shadow lend.   4
Describe Adonis, and the counterfeit
Is poorly imitated after you;
On Helen's cheek all art of beauty set,
And you in Grecian tires are painted new: 8
Speak of the spring and foison of the year,
The one doth shadow of your beauty show,
The other as your bounty doth appear;
And you in every blessed shape we know.   12
    In all external grace you have some part,
    But you like none, none you, for constant heart.

54

O, how much more doth beauty beauteous seem
By that sweet ornament which truth doth give!
The rose looks fair, but fairer we it deem
For that sweet odour which doth in it live.   4
The canker-blooms have full as deep a dye
As the perfumed tincture of the roses,
Hang on such thorns, and play as wantonly
When summer's breath their masked buds discloses: 8
But, for their virtue only is their show,
They live unwoo'd, and unrespected fade;
Die to themselves.   Sweet roses do not so;
Of their sweet deaths are sweetest odours made: 12
    And so of you, beauteous and lovely youth,
    When that shall vade, my verse distils your truth.

3 every one, one shade: *one shadow apiece*   5 counterfeit: *portrait*
8 tires: *headdresses*   9 foison: *harvest*   11 bounty: *generosity*
14 like none: *are like none*   none you: *none are like you*
5 canker-blooms: *dog-roses, scentless wild roses*
6 tincture: *color*   8 discloses: *unfolds, opens*
9 only is their show: *consists only in their appearance*
10 unrespected: *unregarded*   11 to themselves: *all alone*
14 that: *that beauty, that youth*   vade: *fade*   distils: *preserves
   the essence of*

55

Not marble, nor the gilded monuments
Of princes, shall outlive this powerful rime;
But you shall shine more bright in these contents
Than unswept stone, besmear'd with sluttish time.   **4**
When wasteful war shall statues overturn,
And broils root out the work of masonry,
Nor Mars his sword nor war's quick fire shall burn
The living record of your memory.   **8**
'Gainst death and all-oblivious enmity
Shall you pace forth; your praise shall still find room
Even in the eyes of all posterity
That wear this world out to the ending doom.   **12**
   So, till the judgment that yourself arise,
    You live in this, and dwell in lovers' eyes.

56

Sweet love, renew thy force; be it not said
Thy edge should blunter be than appetite,
Which but to-day by feeding is allay'd,
To-morrow sharpen'd in his former might: **4**
So, love, be thou; although to-day thou fill
Thy hungry eyes, even till they wink with fulness,
To-morrow see again, and do not kill
The spirit of love with a perpetual dulness.   **8**
Let this sad interim like the ocean be
Which parts the shore, where two contracted new
Come daily to the banks, that, when they see
Return of love, more bless'd may be the view;   **12**
   Or call it winter, which, being full of care,
    Makes summer's welcome thrice more wish'd, more
     rare.

---

7 Nor Mars his: *neither Mars'*
12 wear this world out: *outlast this world*   ending doom: *to the*
   judgment day that ends all
13 that: *when*   10 contracted new: *but lately betrothed*

57

Being your slave, what should I do but tend
Upon the hours and times of your desire?
I have no precious time at all to spend,
Nor services to do, till you require.   4
Nor dare I chide the world-without-end hour
Whilst I, my sovereign, watch the clock for you,
Nor think the bitterness of absence sour
When you have bid your servant once adieu;   8
Nor dare I question with my jealous thought
Where you may be, or your affairs suppose,
But, like a sad slave, stay and think of nought,
Save where you are how happy you make those.   12
   So true a fool is love that in your will,
   Though you do anything, he thinks no ill.

58

That god forbid that made me first your slave,
I should in thought control your times of pleasure,
Or at your hand the account of hours to crave,
Being your vassal, bound to stay your leisure!   4
O, let me suffer, being at your beck,
The imprison'd absence of your liberty;
And patience, tame to sufferance, bide each check,
Without accusing you of injury.   8
Be where you list, your charter is so strong
That you yourself may privilege your time
To what you will; to you it doth belong
Yourself to pardon of self-doing crime.   12
   I am to wait, though waiting so be hell,
   Not blame your pleasure, be it ill or well.

---

5 world-without-end: *never ending*   10 suppose: *conjecture*
6 The imprison'd . . . liberty; *cf. n.*
7 sufferance: *suffering*   check: *rebuke*
10 privilege: *authorize*   12 self-doing: *done by yourself*

59

If there be nothing new, but that which is
Hath been before, how are our brains beguil'd,
Which, labouring for invention, bear amiss
The second burden of a former child!   4
O, that record could with a backward look,
Even of five hundred courses of the sun,
Show me your image in some antique book,
Since mind at first in character was done!   8
That I might see what the old world could say
To this composed wonder of your frame;
Whether we are mended, or whe'r better they,
Or whether revolution be the same.   12

   O, sure I am, the wits of former days
   To subjects worse have given admiring praise.

60

Like as the waves make towards the pebbled shore,
So do our minutes hasten to their end;
Each changing place with that which goes before,
In sequent toil all forwards do contend.   4
Nativity, once in the main of light,
Crawls to maturity, wherewith being crown'd,
Crooked eclipses 'gainst his glory fight,
And Time that gave doth now his gift confound.   8
Time doth transfix the flourish set on youth
And delves the parallels in beauty's brow,
Feeds on the rarities of nature's truth,
And nothing stands but for his scythe to mow: 12

   And yet to times in hope my verse shall stand,
   Praising thy worth, despite his cruel hand.

3 labouring for invention: *striving for originality*   5 record: *memory*
8 in character: *in letters*   10 composed wonder: *wonderful composition*
11 mended: *advanced beyond our predecessors*   whe'r: *whether*
12 whether revolution be the same: *whether all things come round
again*   4 In sequent toil . . . contend; *cf. n.*   5 main: *flood*
7 Crooked: *malignant*
9 transfix the flourish: *remove the embellishment*
10 delves the parallels: *digs wrinkles*   13 times in hope: *future times*

61

Is it thy will thy image should keep open
My heavy eyelids to the weary night?
Dost thou desire my slumbers should be broken,
While shadows, like to thee, do mock my sight? 4
Is it thy spirit that thou send'st from thee
So far from home, into my deeds to pry,
To find out shames and idle hours in me,
The scope and tenour of thy jealousy? 8
O, no! thy love, though much, is not so great:
It is my love that keeps mine eye awake;
Mine own true love that doth my rest defeat,
To play the watchman ever for thy sake: 12
 For thee watch I whilst thou dost wake elsewhere,
 From me far off, with others all too near.

62

Sin of self-love possesseth all mine eye
And all my soul and all my every part;
And for this sin there is no remedy,
It is so grounded inward in my heart. 4
Methinks no face so gracious is as mine,
No shape so true, no truth of such account;
And for myself mine own worth do define,
As I all other in all worths surmount. 8
But when my glass shows me myself indeed,
Beated and chopp'd with tann'd antiquity,
Mine own self-love quite contrary I read;
Self so self-loving were iniquity. 12
 'Tis thee, myself,—that for myself I praise,
 Painting my age with beauty of thy days.

8 scope and tenour: *aim and substance*   11 defeat: *destroy*
7 do define: *I do define*   8 As: *so that*   other: *others*
10 Beated and chopp'd: *battered (?) and chapped; cf. n.*
 antiquity: *old age*

63

Against my love shall be, as I am now,
With Time's injurious hand crush'd and o'erworn;
When hours have drain'd his blood and fill'd his brow
With lines and wrinkles; when his youthful morn   4
Hath travell'd on to age's steepy night;
And all those beauties whereof now he's king
Are vanishing or vanish'd out of sight,
Stealing away the treasure of his spring;   8
For such a time do I now fortify
Against confounding age's cruel knife,
That he shall never cut from memory
My sweet love's beauty, though my lover's life: 12
     His beauty shall in these black lines be seen,
     And they shall live, and he in them still green.

64

When I have seen by Time's fell hand defac'd
The rich-proud cost of outworn buried age;
When sometime lofty towers I see down-raz'd,
And brass eternal slave to mortal rage;   4
When I have seen the hungry ocean gain
Advantage on the kingdom of the shore,
And the firm soil win of the watery main,
Increasing store with loss, and loss with store;   8
When I have seen such interchange of state,
Or state itself confounded to decay;
Ruin hath taught me thus to ruminate—
That Time will come and take my love away.   12
     This thought is as a death, which cannot choose
     But weep to have that which it fears to lose.

1 **Against:** *when, in anticipation of the time when*
5 **steepy:** *steep, surmounted with difficulty*
10 **confounding:** *destroying*   12 **though:** *though he cuts*
2 **rich-proud . . . age:** *costly and splendid tombs or monuments*
3 **sometime:** *once, formerly*
4 **brass eternal slave:** *eternal brass the slave*
9 **state:** *condition of things*   10 **state itself:** *grandeur*
13 **which:** *this thought which*

65

Since brass, nor stone, nor earth, nor boundless sea,
But sad mortality o'ersways their power,
How with this rage shall beauty hold a plea,
Whose action is no stronger than a flower? 4
O, how shall summer's honey breath hold out
Against the wrackful siege of battering days,
When rocks impregnable are not so stout,
Nor gates of steel so strong, but Time decays? 8
O fearful meditation! where, alack,
Shall Time's best jewel from Time's chest lie hid?
Or what strong hand can hold his swift foot back?
Or who his spoil of beauty can forbid? 12
   O, none, unless this miracle have might,
   That in black ink my love may still shine bright.

66

Tir'd with all these, for restful death I cry
As to behold desert a beggar born,
And needy nothing trimm'd in jollity,
And purest faith unhappily forsworn, 4
And gilded honour shamefully misplac'd,
And maiden virtue rudely strumpeted,
And right perfection wrongfully disgrac'd,
And strength by limping sway disabled, 8
And art made tongue-tied by authority,
And folly—doctor-like—controlling skill,
And simple truth miscall'd simplicity,
And captive good attending captain ill: 12
   Tir'd with all these, from these would I be gone,
   Save that to die, I leave my love alone.

1 Since: *since there is not*   4 action: *vigor*
6 wrackful: *destructive*   12 spoil: *plundering*
3 needy nothing: *empty vanity*   trimm'd in jollity: *decked in finery*
4 unhappily forsworn: *unluckily frustrated*
5 misplac'd: *bestowed amiss*   8 disabled: *rendered helpless*
11 simplicity: *folly*   14 to die: *by dying*

67

Ah! wherefore with infection should he live,
And with his presence grace impiety,
That sin by him advantage should achieve,
And lace itself with his society?   **4**
Why should false painting imitate his cheek,
And steal dead seeing of his living hue?
Why should poor beauty indirectly seek
Roses of shadow, since his rose is true?   **8**
Why should he live, now Nature bankrupt is,
Beggar'd of blood to blush through lively veins?
For she hath no exchequer now but his,
And, proud of many, lives upon his gains.   **12**
    O, him she stores, to show what wealth she had
    In days long since, before these last so bad.

68

Thus is his cheek the map of days outworn,
When beauty liv'd and died as flowers do now,
Before these bastard signs of fair were born,
Or durst inhabit on a living brow;   **4**
Before the golden tresses of the dead,
The right of sepulchres, were shorn away,
To live a second life on second head;
Ere beauty's dead fleece made another gay: **8**
In him those holy antique hours are seen,
Without all ornament, itself and true,
Making no summer of another's green,
Robbing no old to dress his beauty new;   **12**
    And him as for a map doth Nature store,
    To show false Art what beauty was of yore.

1 with infection: *in this infected world*   4 lace itself: *decorate itself*
6 dead seeing: *a dead appearance*   7 indirectly; *cf. n.*
13 stores: *treasures up*   1 map: *picture*   3 bastard signs of fair; *cf. n.*
6 The right of sepulchres: *property belonging to the tomb*
9 antique hours: *hours of antiquity*
10 itself and true: *natural and sincere*

69

Those parts of thee that the world's eye doth view
Want nothing that the thought of hearts can mend;
All tongues—the voice of souls—give thee that due,
Uttering bare truth, even so as foes commend.   4
Thy outward thus with outward praise is crown'd;
But those same tongues, that give thee so thine own,
In other accents do this praise confound
By seeing farther than the eye hath shown.   8
They look into the beauty of thy mind,
And that, in guess, they measure by thy deeds;
Then,—churls,—their thoughts, although their eyes
    were kind,
To thy fair flower add the rank smell of weeds: 12
  But why thy odour matcheth not thy show,
  The soil is this, that thou dost common grow.

70

That thou art blam'd shall not be thy defect,
For slander's mark was ever yet the fair;
The ornament of beauty is suspect,
A crow that flies in heaven's sweetest air.   4
So thou be good, slander doth but approve
Thy worth the greater, being woo'd of time;
For canker vice the sweetest buds doth love,
And thou present'st a pure unstained prime.   8
Thou hast pass'd by the ambush of young days,
Either not assail'd, or victor being charg'd;
Yet this thy praise cannot be so thy praise,
To tie up envy evermore enlarg'd: 12
  If some suspect of ill mask'd not thy show,
  Then thou alone kingdoms of hearts shouldst owe.

14 soil; *cf. n.*   common: *too accessible*   1-14 *Cf. n.*
3 ornament: *identifying badge*   suspect: *suspicion, distrust*
5 approve: *prove*   6 woo'd of time: *wooed by the world*
8 prime: *spring, youth*   10 charg'd: *attacked*
11 so thy praise: *so much thy praise*
12 To tie up: *that it will tie up*   enlarg'd: *at liberty*
13 mask'd not thy show: *did not disfigure your beauty*   14 owe: *own*

71

No longer mourn for me when I am dead
Than you shall hear the surly sullen bell
Give warning to the world that I am fled
From this vile world, with vilest worms to dwell: 4
Nay, if you read this line, remember not
The hand that writ it; for I love you so,
That I in your sweet thoughts would be forgot,
If thinking on me then should make you woe.   8
O, if, I say, you look upon this verse,
When I perhaps compounded am with clay,
Do not so much as my poor name rehearse,
But let your love even with my life decay;   12
    Lest the wise world should look into your moan,
    And mock you with me after I am gone.

72

O, lest the world should task you to recite
What merit lived in me, that you should love
After my death,—dear love, forget me quite,
For you in me can nothing worthy prove;   4
Unless you would devise some virtuous lie,
To do more for me than mine own desert,
And hang more praise upon deceased I
Than niggard truth would willingly impart: 8
O, lest your true love may seem false in this,
That you for love speak well of me untrue,
My name be buried where my body is,
And live no more to shame nor me nor you.   12
    For I am sham'd by that which I bring forth,
    And so should you, to love things nothing worth.

3 Give warning to the world; *cf. n.*   7 would be: *wish to be*
10 compounded: *mixed*   11 rehearse: *repeat*   1 task: *challenge*
4 prove: *discover*   10 untrue: *untruly*
11 My name: *let my name*   14 should you: *should you be shamed*

73

That time of year thou mayst in me behold
When yellow leaves, or none, or few, do hang
Upon those boughs which shake against the cold,
Bare ruin'd choirs, where late the sweet birds sang.   4
In me thou see'st the twilight of such day
As after sunset fadeth in the west;
Which by and by black night doth take away,
Death's second self, that seals up all in rest.   8
In me thou see'st the glowing of such fire,
That on the ashes of his youth doth lie,
As the death-bed whereon it must expire,
Consum'd with that which it was nourish'd by.   12
   This thou perceiv'st, which makes thy love more strong,
   To love that well which thou must leave ere long.

74

But be contented: when that fell arrest
Without all bail shall carry me away,
My life hath in this line some interest,
Which for memorial still with thee shall stay.   4
When thou reviewest this, thou dost review
The very part was consecrate to thee:
The earth can have but earth, which is his due;
My spirit is thine, the better part of me: 8
So then thou hast but lost the dregs of life,
The prey of worms, my body being dead;
The coward conquest of a wretch's knife,
Too base of thee to be remembered.   12
   The worth of that is that which it contains,
   And that is this, and this with thee remains.

12 Consum'd with that . . . nourish'd by; *cf. n.*
3 interest: *claim, part*   4 Which: *this line which*
5 reviewest: *surveyest*   6 was consecrate: *that was consecrated*
12 of thee: *by thee*
13 of that: *of that body*   is that: *is that spirit*
14 that is this: *that spirit is this poetry*

75

So are you to my thoughts as food to life,
Or as sweet-season'd showers are to the ground;
And for the peace of you I hold such strife
As 'twixt a miser and his wealth is found;   4
Now proud as an enjoyer, and anon
Doubting the filching age will steal his treasure;
Now counting best to be with you alone,
Then better'd that the world may see my pleasure: 8
Sometime all full with feasting on your sight,
And by and by clean starved for a look;
Possessing or pursuing no delight,
Save what is had or must from you be took.   12
    Thus do I pine and surfeit day by day,
    Or gluttoning on all, or all away.

76

Why is my verse so barren of new pride,
So far from variation or quick change?
Why with the time do I not glance aside
To new-found methods and to compounds strange?   4
Why write I still all one, ever the same,
And keep invention in a noted weed,
That every word doth almost tell my name,
Showing their birth, and where they did proceed?   8
O, know, sweet love, I always write of you,
And you and love are still my argument;
So all my best is dressing old words new,
Spending again what is already spent: 12
    For as the sun is daily new and old,
    So is my love still telling what is told.

2 sweet-season'd: *mild*   3 peace of you: *peaceful possession of you*
6 Doubting: *fearing*
8 better'd that: *made happier, more fortunate, because*
12 had: *had from you*
14 Or: *either*   or all away: *or putting all aside, refusing all*
1 new pride: *ostentatious novelty*   6 noted weed: *well-known dress*

77

Thy glass will show thee how thy beauties wear,
Thy dial how thy precious minutes waste;
The vacant leaves thy mind's imprint will bear,
And of this book this learning mayst thou taste.   **4**
The wrinkles which thy glass will truly show
Of mouthed graves will give thee memory;
Thou by thy dial's shady stealth mayst know
Time's thievish progress to eternity.   **8**
Look! what thy memory cannot contain,
Commit to these waste blanks, and thou shalt **find**
Those children nurs'd, deliver'd from thy brain,
To take a new acquaintance of thy mind.   **12**
   These offices, so oft as thou wilt look,
   Shall profit thee and much enrich thy book.

78

So oft have I invok'd thee for my Muse
And found such fair assistance in my verse
As every alien pen hath got my use
And under thee their poesy disperse.   **4**
Thine eyes, that taught the dumb on high to sing
And heavy ignorance aloft to fly,
Have added feathers to the learned's wing
And given grace a double majesty.   **8**
Yet be most proud of that which I compile,
Whose influence is thine, and born of thee:
In others' works thou dost but mend the style,
And arts with thy sweet graces graced be;   **12**
   But thou art all my art, and dost advance
   As high as learning my rude ignorance.

1-14 *Cf. n.*   4 *Cf. n.*   7 shady stealth: *stealthy shadow*
10 waste blanks: *empty pages*   11, 12 *Cf. n.*   13 offices; *cf. n.*
1-14 *Cf. n.*   3 As: *that*   use: *habit*
4 under thee: *under thy patronage*   disperse: *spread abroad*
9 compile: *compose*   10 influence: *inspiration*   13 advance: *raise*

79

Whilst I alone did call upon thy aid,
My verse alone had all thy gentle grace;
But now my gracious numbers are decay'd,
And my sick muse doth give another place.   4
I grant, sweet love, thy lovely argument
Deserves the travail of a worthier pen;
Yet what of thee thy poet doth invent
He robs thee of, and pays it thee again.   8
He lends thee virtue, and he stole that word
From thy behaviour; beauty doth he give,
And found it in thy cheek; he can afford
No praise to thee but what in thee doth live.   12
 Then thank him not for that which he doth say,
 Since what he owes thee thou thyself dost pay.

80

O, how I faint when I of you do write,
Knowing a better spirit doth use your name,
And in the praise thereof spends all his might,
To make me tongue-tied, speaking of your fame!   4
But since your worth,—wide as the ocean is,—
The humble as the proudest sail doth bear,
My saucy bark, inferior far to his,
On your broad main doth wilfully appear.   8
Your shallowest help will hold me up afloat,
Whilst he upon your soundless deep doth ride;
Or, being wrack'd, I am a worthless boat,
He of tall building and of goodly pride: 12
 Then if he thrive and I be cast away,
 The worst was this;—my love was my decay.

4 give another place: *yield to another*
5 thy . . . argument: *the theme of your beauty*
2 a better spirit; *cf. n.*   8 wilfully: *eagerly*
11 wrack'd: *wrecked*

81

Or I shall live your epitaph to make,
Or you survive when I in earth am rotten;
From hence your memory death cannot take,
Although in me each part will be forgotten. 4
Your name from hence immortal life shall have,
Though I, once gone, to all the world must die:
The earth can yield me but a common grave,
When you entombed in men's eyes shall lie. 8
Your monument shall be my gentle verse,
Which eyes not yet created shall o'er-read;
And tongues to be your being shall rehearse,
When all the breathers of this world are dead; 12
    You still shall live,—such virtue hath my pen,—
    Where breath most breathes,—even in the mouths of
      men.

82

I grant thou wert not married to my Muse,
And therefore mayst without attaint o'erlook
The dedicated words which writers use
Of their fair subject, blessing every book. 4
Thou art as fair in knowledge as in hue,
Finding thy worth a limit past my praise;
And therefore art enforc'd to seek anew
Some fresher stamp of the time-bettering days. 8
And do so, love; yet when they have devis'd
What strained touches rhetoric can lend,
Thou truly fair wert truly sympathiz'd
In true plain words by thy true-telling friend; 12
    And their gross painting might be better us'd
    Where cheeks need blood; in thee it is abus'd.

6 to all the world: *in the world's memory*
11 to be: *of future generations*   2 attaint: *disgrace*
6 limit: *mark, goal*   8 time-bettering days: *present greater age*
10 strained: *exaggerated*   11 sympathiz'd: *matched*

83

I never saw that you did painting need,
And therefore to your fair no painting set;
I found, or thought I found, you did exceed
The barren tender of a poet's debt: 4
And therefore have I slept in your report,
That you yourself, being extant, well might show
How far a modern quill doth come too short,
Speaking of worth, what worth in you doth grow.   8
This silence for my sin you did impute,
Which shall be most my glory, being dumb;
For I impair not beauty being mute,
When others would give life, and bring a tomb.   12
   There lives more life in one of your fair eyes
   Than both your poets can in praise devise.

84

Who is it that says most, which can say more
Than this rich praise,—that you alone are you,
In whose confine immured is the store
Which should example where your equal grew?   4
Lean penury within that pen doth dwell
That to his subject lends not some small glory;
But he that writes of you, if he can tell
That you are you, so dignifies his story.   8
Let him but copy what in you is writ,
Not making worse what nature made so clear,
And such a counterpart shall fame his wit,
Making his style admired everywhere.   12
   You to your beauteous blessings add a curse,
      Being fond on praise, which makes your praises
         worse.

4 tender: *offer to pay*   5 in your report: *in describing, praising, you*
7 modern: *ordinary*   14 both your poets; *cf. n.*
3, 4 In whose confine . . . equal grew; *cf. n.*   10 clear: *glorious*
11 counterpart: *reproduction*   fame: *give fame to*
13 beauteous blessings: *blessings of beauty*
14 Being fond . . . praises worse; *cf. n.*

85

My tongue-tied Muse in manners holds her still,
Whilst comments of your praise, richly compil'd,
Reserve their character with golden quill,
And precious phrase by all the Muses fil'd.   4
I think good thoughts, while others write good words,
And, like unletter'd clerk, still cry 'Amen'
To every hymn that able spirit affords
In polish'd form of well-refined pen.   8
Hearing you prais'd, I say, ' 'Tis so, 'tis true,'
And to the most of praise add something more;
But that is in my thought, whose love to you,
Though words come hindmost, holds his rank before. 12
    Then others for the breath of words respect,
    Me for my dumb thoughts, speaking in effect.

86

Was it the proud full sail of his great verse,
Bound for the prize of all too precious you,
That did my ripe thoughts in my brain inhearse,
Making their tomb the womb wherein they grew?   4
Was it his spirit, by spirits taught to write
Above a mortal pitch, that struck me dead?
No, neither he, nor his compeers by night
Giving him aid, my verse astonished.   8
He, nor that affable familiar ghost
Which nightly gulls him with intelligence,
As victors of my silence cannot boast;
I was not sick of any fear from thence: 12
    But when your countenance fill'd up his line,
    Then lack'd I matter; that enfeebled mine.

1 in manners: *modestly*
2 richly compil'd: *composed in an elaborate style*
3 Reserve their character; *cf. n.*
4 precious: *carefully wrought*   fil'd: *polished*
7 that able spirit; *cf. n.*
12 Though words . . . before; *cf. n.*   rank: *place in line*
13 respect: *esteem*   14 speaking in effect: *which virtually speak*
3 inhearse: *lay as in a coffin*   8 astonished: *dismayed*
10 gulls: *cheats*   13 countenance: *favor*

87

Farewell! thou art too dear for my possessing,
And like enough thou know'st thy estimate:
The charter of thy worth gives thee releasing;
My bonds in thee are all determinate.   4
For how do I hold thee but by thy granting?
And for that riches where is my deserving?
The cause of this fair gift in me is wanting,
And so my patent back again is swerving.   8
Thyself thou gav'st, thy own worth then not knowing,
Or me, to whom thou gav'st it, else mistaking;
So thy great gift, upon misprision growing,
Comes home again, on better judgment making.   12
 Thus have I had thee, as a dream doth flatter,
 In sleep a king, but, waking, no such matter.

88

When thou shalt be dispos'd to set me light,
And place my merit in the eye of scorn,
Upon thy side against myself I'll fight,
And prove thee virtuous, though thou art forsworn.   4
With mine own weakness being best acquainted,
Upon thy part I can set down a story
Of faults conceal'd, wherein I am attainted;
That thou in losing me shalt win much glory: 8
And I by this will be a gainer too;
For bending all my loving thoughts on thee,
The injuries that to myself I do,
Doing thee vantage, double-vantage me.   12
 Such is my love, to thee I so belong,
 That for thy right myself will bear all wrong.

2 estimate: *value* 3 *Cf. n.* 4 determinate: *expired*
8 patent: *conditional privilege* swerving: *turning from me*
11 upon misprision growing: *made mistakenly*
1 set me light: *estimate me lightly* 6 Upon thy part: *in your behalf*
12 double-vantage: *doubly reward*

89

Say that thou didst forsake me for some fault,
And I will comment upon that offence:
Speak of my lameness, and I straight will halt,
Against thy reasons making no defence.   4
Thou canst not, love, disgrace me half so ill,
To set a form upon desired change,
As I'll myself disgrace; knowing thy will,
I will acquaintance strangle, and look strange;   8
Be absent from thy walks; and in my tongue
Thy sweet beloved name no more shall dwell,
Lest I, too much profane, should do it wrong,
And haply of our old acquaintance tell.   12
    For thee, against myself I'll vow debate,
    For I must ne'er love him whom thou dost hate.

90

Then hate me when thou wilt; if ever, now;
Now, while the world is bent my deeds to cross,
Join with the spite of fortune, make me bow,
And do not drop in for an after-loss: 4
Ah! do not, when my heart hath 'scap'd this sorrow,
Come in the rearward of a conquer'd woe;
Give not a windy night a rainy morrow,
To linger out a purpos'd overthrow.   8
If thou wilt leave me, do not leave me last,
When other petty griefs have done their spite,
But in the onset come: so shall I taste
At first the very worst of fortune's might;   12
    And other strains of woe, which now seem woe,
    Compar'd with loss of thee will not seem so.

2 comment: *discourse*
6 set a form: *put a good semblance*   upon desired change: *on the*
  change you wish in our relations
8 acquaintance strangle: *end our acquaintance*   look strange:
  assume the air of a stranger   12 haply: *perchance*
13 debate: *strife*   2 cross: *thwart*
4 drop in: *come in suddenly*   6 *Cf. n.*   8 linger out: *prolong*
11 onset: *first attack*   13 strains: *emotions*

91

Some glory in their birth, some in their skill,
Some in their wealth, some in their body's force;
Some in their garments, though new-fangled ill;
Some in their hawks and hounds, some in their horse; 4
And every humour hath his adjunct pleasure,
Wherein it finds a joy above the rest:
But these particulars are not my measure;
All these I better in one general best. 8
Thy love is better than high birth to me,
Richer than wealth, prouder than garments' cost,
Of more delight than hawks or horses be;
And having thee, of all men's pride I boast: 12
    Wretched in this alone, that thou mayst take
    All this away, and me most wretched make.

92

But do thy worst to steal thyself away,
For term of life thou art assured mine;
And life no longer than thy love will stay,
For it depends upon that love of thine. 4
Then need I not to fear the worst of wrongs,
When in the least of them my life hath end.
I see a better state to me belongs
Than that which on thy humour doth depend: 8
Thou canst not vex me with inconstant mind,
Since that my life on thy revolt doth lie.
O! what a happy title do I find,
Happy to have thy love, happy to die: 12
    But what's so blessed-fair that fears no blot?
    Thou mayst be false, and yet I know it not.

3 new-fangled ill: *fashionably ugly*
5 humour: *disposition*   adjunct: *connected*
7 measure: *limit (of joy)*   8 humour: *mood*
10 Since that . . . lie: *since my life would end if you betrayed me*

93

So shall I live, supposing thou art true,
Like a deceived husband; so love's face
May still seem love to me, though alter'd new,
Thy looks with me, thy heart in other place: 4
For there can live no hatred in thine eye,
Therefore in that I cannot know thy change.
In many's looks the false heart's history
Is writ in moods, and frowns, and wrinkles strange,   8
But heaven in thy creation did decree
That in thy face sweet love should ever dwell;
Whate'er thy thoughts or thy heart's workings be,
Thy looks should nothing thence but sweetness tell. 12
　　How like Eve's apple doth thy beauty grow,
　　If thy sweet virtue answer not thy show!

94

They that have power to hurt and will do none,
That do not do the thing they most do show,
Who, moving others, are themselves as stone,
Unmoved, cold, and to temptation slow;   4
They rightly do inherit heaven's graces,
And husband nature's riches from expense;
They are the lords and owners of their faces,
Others but stewards of their excellence.   8
The summer's flower is to the summer sweet,
Though to itself it only live and die,
But if that flower with base infection meet,
The basest weed outbraves his dignity: 12
　　For sweetest things turn sourest by their deeds;
　　Lilies that fester smell far worse than weeds.

94. 1-14 *Cf. n.*　　　　　　　　　　　　　　　2 show: *seem to do*
6 husband . . . expense: *do not squander nature's gifts in passion*
9-12 *Cf. n.*　　　　　　　　　　　　　　　　　14 *Cf. n.*

95

How sweet and lovely dost thou make the shame
Which, like a canker in the fragrant rose,
Doth spot the beauty of thy budding name!
O, in what sweets dost thou thy sins enclose!   4
That tongue that tells the story of thy days,
Making lascivious comments on thy sport,
Cannot dispraise but in a kind of praise;
Naming thy name blesses an ill report.   8
O, what a mansion have those vices got
Which for their habitation chose out thee,
Where beauty's veil doth cover every blot
And all things turn to fair that eyes can see!   12
    Take heed, dear heart, of this large privilege;
    The hardest knife ill-us'd doth lose his edge.

96

Some say thy fault is youth, some wantonness;
Some say thy grace is youth and gentle sport;
Both grace and faults are lov'd of more and less:
Thou mak'st faults graces that to thee resort.   4
As on the finger of a throned queen
The basest jewel will be well esteem'd,
So are those errors that in thee are seen
To truths translated and for true things deem'd.   8
How many lambs might the stern wolf betray,
If like a lamb he could his looks translate!
How many gazers mightst thou lead away,
If thou wouldst use the strength of all thy state!   12
    But do not so; I love thee in such sort,
    As, thou being mine, mine is thy good report.

2 canker: *cankerworm*   13 privilege: *license*
3 more and less: *high and low*   8 translated: *changed*
12 state: *grandeur, beauty* (*?*)   13, 14 *Cf. n.*

97

How like a winter hath my absence been
From thee, the pleasure of the fleeting year!
What freezings have I felt, what dark days seen!
What old December's bareness everywhere! 4
And yet this time remov'd was summer's time,
The teeming autumn, big with rich increase,
Bearing the wanton burden of the prime,
Like widow'd wombs after their lords' decease: 8
Yet this abundant issue seem'd to me
But hope of orphans and unfather'd fruit;
For summer and his pleasures wait on thee,
And, thou away, the very birds are mute: 12
    Or, if they sing, 'tis with so dull a cheer,
    That leaves look pale, dreading the winter's near.

98

From you have I been absent in the spring,
When proud-pied April, dress'd in all his trim,
Hath put a spirit of youth in everything,
That heavy Saturn laugh'd and leap'd with him. 4
Yet nor the lays of birds, nor the sweet smell
Of different flowers in odour and in hue,
Could make me any summer's story tell,
Or from their proud lap pluck them where they grew:
Nor did I wonder at the lily's white, 9
Nor praise the deep vermilion in the rose;
They were but sweet, but figures of delight,
Drawn after you, you pattern of all those. 12
    Yet seem'd it winter still, and, you away,
    As with your shadow I with these did play.

5 time remov'd: *time of absence*   13 cheer: *mood*
2 proud-pied: *magnificent in many colors*   trim: *finery*
4 heavy Saturn: *Saturn, god of heaviness or melancholy*
7 summer's story: *pleasant tale*   9 wonder at: *admire*

99

The forward violet thus did I chide:
Sweet thief, whence didst thou steal thy sweet that
    smells,
If not from my love's breath? The purple pride
Which on thy soft cheek for complexion dwells   4
In my love's veins thou hast too grossly dy'd.
The lily I condemned for thy hand,
And buds of marjoram had stol'n thy hair;
The roses fearfully on thorns did stand,   8
One blushing shame, another white despair;
A third, nor red nor white, had stol'n of both,
And to his robbery had annex'd thy breath;
But, for his theft, in pride of all his growth   12
A vengeful canker eat him up to death.
    More flowers I noted, yet I none could see
    But sweet or colour it had stol'n from thee.

100

Where art thou, Muse, that thou forget'st so long
To speak of that which gives thee all thy might?
Spend'st thou thy fury on some worthless song,
Darkening thy power to lend base subjects light?   4
Return, forgetful Muse, and straight redeem
In gentle numbers time so idly spent;
Sing to the ear that doth thy lays esteem
And gives thy pen both skill and argument.   8
Rise, resty Muse, my love's sweet face survey,
If Time have any wrinkle graven there;
If any, be a satire to decay,
And make Time's spoils despised everywhere.   12
    Give my love fame faster than Time wastes life;
    So thou prevent'st his scythe and crooked knife.

1 forward: *early*   5 grossly: *obviously*   6 for: *compared with*
7 buds of marjoram; *cf. n.*   3 fury: *inspiration*   9 resty: *indolent*
11 be . . . decay: *satirize Time's destruction of beauty*
14 prevent'st: *forestall'st*

101

O truant Muse, what shall be thy amends
For thy neglect of truth in beauty dy'd?
Both truth and beauty on my love depends;
So dost thou too, and therein dignified.   4
Make answer, Muse: wilt thou not haply say,
'Truth needs no colour, with his colour fix'd;
Beauty no pencil, beauty's truth to lay;
But best is best, if never intermix'd'?   8
Because he needs no praise, wilt thou be dumb?
Excuse not silence so; for 't lies in thee
To make him much outlive a gilded tomb
And to be prais'd of ages yet to be.   12
    Then do thy office, Muse; I teach thee how
    To make him seem long hence as he shows now.

102

My love is strengthen'd, though more weak in seeming;
I love not less, though less the show appear:
That love is merchandiz'd whose rich esteeming
The owner's tongue doth publish everywhere.   4
Our love was new, and then but in the spring,
When I was wont to greet it with my lays;
As Philomel in summer's front doth sing,
And stops her pipe in growth of riper days: 8
Not that the summer is less pleasant now
Than when her mournful hymns did hush the night,
But that wild music burthens every bough,
And sweets grown common lose their dear delight.   12
    Therefore, like her, I sometime hold my tongue,
    Because I would not dull you with my song.

---

4 dignified: *art dignified*   7 lay: *apply, as a color*
8 if never intermix'd: *if left to itself*   13 office: *work*
1 seeming: *appearance*
3 merchandiz'd: *cheapened*   esteeming: *worth*
7 Philomel: *the nightingale*   front: *beginning*

103

Alack! what poverty my Muse brings forth,
That having such a scope to show her pride,
The argument, all bare, is of more worth
Than when it hath my added praise beside!   4
O, blame me not, if I no more can write!
Look in your glass, and there appears a face
That over-goes my blunt invention quite,
Dulling my lines and doing me disgrace.   8
Were it not sinful then, striving to mend,
To mar the subject that before was well?
For to no other pass my verses tend
Than of your graces and your gifts to tell;   12
    And more, much more, than in my verse can sit,
    Your own glass shows you when you look in it.

104

To me, fair friend, you never can be old,
For as you were when first your eye I ey'd,
Such seems your beauty still. Three winters cold
Have from the forests shook three summers' pride, 4
Three beauteous springs to yellow autumn turn'd
In process of the seasons have I seen,
Three April perfumes in three hot Junes burn'd,
Since first I saw you fresh, which yet are green. 8
Ah! yet doth beauty, like a dial-hand,
Steal from his figure, and no pace perceiv'd;
So your sweet hue, which methinks still doth stand,
Hath motion, and mine eye may be deceiv'd: 12
    For fear of which, hear this, thou age unbred:
    Ere you were born was beauty's summer dead.

11 pass: *end*   13 sit: *be contained*
6 process: *procession*   9 dial-hand: *hand of a watch*

105

Let not my love be call'd idolatry,
Nor my beloved as an idol show,
Since all alike my songs and praises be
To one, of one, still such, and ever so.   4
Kind is my love to-day, to-morrow kind,
Still constant in a wondrous excellence;
Therefore my verse, to constancy confin'd,
One thing expressing, leaves out difference.   8
'Fair, kind, and true,' is all my argument,
'Fair, kind, and true,' varying to other words;
And in this change is my invention spent,
Three themes in one, which wondrous scope affords. 12
   'Fair, kind, and true' have often liv'd alone,
   Which three till now never kept seat in one.

106

When in the chronicle of wasted time
I see descriptions of the fairest wights,
And beauty making beautiful old rime,
In praise of ladies dead and lovely knights,   4
Then, in the blazon of sweet beauty's best,
Of hand, of foot, of lip, of eye, of brow,
I see their antique pen would have express'd
Even such a beauty as you master now.   8
So all their praises are but prophecies
Of this our time, all you prefiguring;
And, for they look'd but with divining eyes,
They had not skill enough your worth to sing: 12
   For we, which now behold these present days,
   Have eyes to wonder, but lack tongues to praise.

2 show: *appear*   8 difference: *variety*
10 varying to other words: *the thought expressed in other words*
5 blazon: *proclaiming*   8 master: *possess*
11 divining: *prophesying*

107

Not mine own fears, nor the prophetic soul
Of the wide world dreaming on things to come,
Can yet the lease of my true love control,
Suppos'd as forfeit to a confin'd doom.   4
The mortal moon hath her eclipse endur'd,
And the sad augurs mock their own presage;
Incertainties now crown themselves assur'd,
And peace proclaims olives of endless age.   8
Now with the drops of this most balmy time
My love looks fresh, and Death to me subscribes,
Since, spite of him, I'll live in this poor rime,
While he insults o'er dull and speechless tribes: 12
  And thou in this shalt find thy monument,
  When tyrants' crests and tombs of brass are spent.

108

What's in the brain, that ink may character,
Which hath not figur'd to thee my true spirit?
What's new to speak, what new to register,
That may express my love, or thy dear merit?   4
Nothing, sweet boy; but yet, like prayers divine,
I must each day say o'er the very same;
Counting no old thing old, thou mine, I thine,
Even as when first I hallow'd thy fair name.   8
So that eternal love in love's fresh case
Weighs not the dust and injury of age,
Nor gives to necessary wrinkles place,
But makes antiquity for aye his page;   12
  Finding the first conceit of love there bred,
  Where time and outward form would show it dead.

1-4 *Cf. n.* 5 mortal: *deadly (?); cf. n.* 6 presage: *presentimen*
10 subscribes: *submits*   13 in this: *in this vers*
1 character: *write*   3 register: *recor*
9 in love's fresh case: *always renewed*
11 gives . . . place: *withdraws when wrinkles must come*
13, 14 *Cf. n.*

109

O, never say that I was false of heart,
Though absence seem'd my flame to qualify.
As easy might I from myself depart
As from my soul, which in thy breast doth lie: 4
That is my home of love: if I have rang'd,
Like him that travels, I return again;
Just to the time, not with the time exchang'd,
So that myself bring water for my stain.   8
Never believe, though in my nature reign'd
All frailties that besiege all kinds of blood,
That it could so preposterously be stain'd,
To leave for nothing all thy sum of good;   12
    For nothing this wide universe I call,
    Save thou, my rose; in it thou art my all.

110

Alas! 'tis true I have gone here and there,
And made myself a motley to the view,
Gor'd mine own thoughts, sold cheap what is most dear,
Made old offences of affections new;   4
Most true it is that I have look'd on truth
Askance and strangely; but, by all above,
These blenches gave my heart another youth,
And worse essays prov'd thee my best of love.   8
Now all is done, have what shall have no end:
Mine appetite I never more will grind
On newer proof, to try an older friend,
A god in love, to whom I am confin'd.   12
    Then give me welcome, next my heaven the best,
    Even to thy pure and most most loving breast.

qualify: *moderate*   5 That: *thy breast*
Just to the time: *punctually*   exchang'd: *changed*
myself bring . . . stain: *justify my fault (of absence)*
10 blood: *temperament*   11 preposterously: *unnaturally*
2 Cf. n.   2 motley: *jester*   3 Gor'd: *wounded*
Made old . . . new: *offended in forsaking old friends for new*
blenches: *inconstancies*   gave . . . youth: *brought me back to
youthful love*   8 worse essays: *trials of the worse*
have what . . . end: *take my unending love*   10 grind: *whet*

111

O, for my sake do you with Fortune chide,
The guilty goddess of my harmful deeds,
That did not better for my life provide
Than public means which public manners breeds.   4
Thence comes it that my name receives a brand,
And almost thence my nature is subdu'd
To what it works in, like the dyer's hand:
Pity me, then, and wish I were renew'd;   8
Whilst, like a willing patient, I will drink
Potions of eisel 'gainst my strong infection;
No bitterness that I will bitter think,
Nor double penance, to correct correction.   12
   Pity me, then, dear friend, and I assure ye
   Even that your pity is enough to cure me.

112

Your love and pity doth the impression fill
Which vulgar scandal stamp'd upon my brow;
For what care I who calls me well or ill,
So you o'er-green my bad, my good allow?   4
You are my all-the-world, and I must strive
To know my shames and praises from your tongue;
None else to me, nor I to none alive,
That my steel'd sense or changes right or wrong.   8
In so profound abysm I throw all care
Of other's voices, that my adder's sense
To critic and to flatterer stopped are.
Mark how with my neglect I do dispense: 12
   You are so strongly in my purpose bred,
   That all the world besides methinks are dead.

2 guilty goddess . . . deeds: *goddess guilty of . . . deeds*
5 brand: *stigma*   6 subdu'd: *reduced*   10 eisel: *vinegar*
12 correct correction: *chastise chastisement, make my correction doubly
   sure*   1 impression: *mark, brand*
4 o'er-green: *cover as by a vine or grass*   allow: *approve*
7, 8 *Cf. n.*   10, 11 *Cf. n.*
12 with . . . dispense: *I am indifferent to neglect (by others)*
13 in my purpose bred: *engrafted in my life*   14 besides: *except you*

113

Since I left you, mine eye is in my mind;
And that which governs me to go about
Doth part his function and is partly blind,
Seems seeing, but effectually is out;⠀⠀⠀⠀⠀⠀⠀4
For it no form delivers to the heart
Of bird, of flower, or shape, which it doth latch:
Of his quick objects hath the mind no part,
Nor his own vision holds what it doth catch;⠀⠀⠀8
For if it see the rud'st or gentlest sight,
The most sweet favour or deformed'st creature,
The mountain or the sea, the day or night,
The crow or dove, it shapes them to your feature:⠀12
⠀⠀Incapable of more, replete with you,
⠀⠀My most true mind thus maketh mine untrue.

114

Or whether doth my mind being crown'd with you,
Drink up the monarch's plague, this flattery?
Or whether shall I say mine eye saith true,
And that your love taught it this alchemy,⠀⠀⠀⠀4
To make of monsters and things indigest
Such cherubins as your sweet self resemble,
Creating every bad a perfect best,
As fast as objects to his beams assemble?⠀⠀⠀⠀8
O, 'tis the first, 'tis flattery in my seeing,
And my great mind most kingly drinks it up:
Mine eye well knows what with his gust is 'greeing,
And to his palate doth prepare the cup:⠀⠀⠀⠀⠀12
⠀⠀If it be poison'd, 'tis the lesser sin
⠀⠀That mine eye loves it and doth first begin.

3 Doth part his function: *does but part of its natural work*
4 effectually: *practically*⠀⠀⠀⠀⠀5 it: *my eye*⠀⠀⠀⠀heart: *mind*
6 latch: *catch*⠀⠀⠀⠀7 his: *the eye's*⠀⠀⠀8 his own: *the eye's*
10 favour: *countenance*⠀⠀14 *Cf. n.*⠀⠀1 Or whether doth: *is it true that*
5 indigest: *formless*⠀⠀⠀⠀⠀⠀⠀⠀⠀⠀⠀⠀10 kingly: *like a king*
11 what . . . 'greeing: *what agrees with the mind's taste*
13, 14 *Cf. n.*

115

Those lines that I before have writ do lie,
Even those that said I could not love you dearer:
Yet then my judgment knew no reason why
My most full flame should afterwards burn clearer.   4
But reckoning Time, whose million'd accidents
Creep in 'twixt vows, and change decrees of kings,
Tan sacred beauty, blunt the sharp'st intents,
Divert strong minds to the course of altering things;   8
Alas! why, fearing of Time's tyranny,
Might I not then say, 'Now I love you best,'
When I was certain o'er incertainty,
Crowning the present, doubting of the rest?   12
    Love is a babe; then might I not say so,
    To give full growth to that which still doth grow.

116

Let me not to the marriage of true minds
Admit impediments.   Love is not love
Which alters when it alteration finds,
Or bends with the remover to remove: 4
O, no! it is an ever-fixed mark,
That looks on tempests and is never shaken;
It is the star to every wandering bark,
Whose worth's unknown, although his height be taken.
Love's not Time's fool, though rosy lips and cheeks   9
Within his bending sickle's compass come;
Love alters not with his brief hours and weeks,
But bears it out even to the edge of doom.   12
    If this be error, and upon me prov'd,
    I never writ, nor no man ever lov'd.

5 reckoning: *taking account of*   12 the rest: *the future*
13 so: *'I love you best'*   14 To give: *giving*
4 remover: *inconstant*   remove: *depart*
8 worth: *power, influence*   height: *altitude*
10 his: *Time's*
                                12 edge of doom: *judgment day*

117

Accuse me thus: that I have scanted all
Wherein I should your great deserts repay,
Forgot upon your dearest love to call,
Whereto all bonds do tie me day by day;　　　4
That I have frequent been with unknown minds,
And given to time your own dear-purchas'd right;
That I have hoisted sail to all the winds
Which should transport me furthest from your sight.　8
Book both my wilfulness and errors down,
And on just proof surmise accumulate;
Bring me within the level of your frown,
But shoot not at me in your waken'd hate;　　　12
　　Since my appeal says I did strive to prove
　　The constancy and virtue of your love.

118

Like as, to make our appetites more keen,
With eager compounds we our palate urge;
As, to prevent our maladies unseen,
We sicken to shun sickness when we purge;　　　4
Even so, being full of your ne'er-cloying sweetness,
To bitter sauces did I frame my feeding;
And, sick of welfare, found a kind of meetness
To be diseas'd, ere that there was true needing.　8
Thus policy in love, to anticipate
The ills that were not, grew to faults assur'd,
And brought to medicine a healthful state,
Which, rank of goodness, would by ill be cur'd;　12
　　But thence I learn, and find the lesson true,
　　Drugs poison him that so fell sick of you.

1 scanted: *grudged*　5 frequent: *intimate*　　　unknown: *unimportant*
6 given to time: *wasted*
10 on . . . accumulate: *add suspected to proved offences*
11 level: *aim*　　　　　　　　　　　　　　1 Like as: *just as*
2 eager compounds: *bitter mixtures*　　　palate urge: *stimulate the*
　appetite　　7 welfare: *good health*　　12 rank of: *cloyed with*

119

What potions have I drunk of Siren tears,
Distill'd from limbecks foul as hell within,
Applying fears to hopes, and hopes to fears,
Still losing when I saw myself to win!   4
What wretched errors hath my heart committed,
Whilst it hath thought itself so blessed never!
How have mine eyes out of their spheres been fitted,
In the distraction of this madding fever!   8
O benefit of ill! now I find true
That better is by evil still made better;
And ruin'd love, when it is built anew,
Grows fairer than at first, more strong, far greater.   12
   So I return rebuk'd to my content,
   And gain by ill thrice more than I have spent.

120

That you were once unkind befriends me now,
And for that sorrow, which I then did feel,
Needs must I under my transgression bow,
Unless my nerves were brass or hammer'd steel.   4
For if you were by my unkindness shaken,
As I by yours, you've pass'd a hell of time;
And I, a tyrant, have no leisure taken
To weigh how once I suffer'd in your crime.   8
O, that our night of woe might have remember'd
My deepest sense, how hard true sorrow hits,
And soon to you, as you to me, then tender'd
The humble salve which wounded bosoms fits!   12
   But that your trespass now becomes a fee;
   Mine ransoms yours, and yours must ransom me.

2 limbecks: *alembics, vessels for distillation*
4 Still . . . win: *winning new loves but losing the old*
7 How . . . fitted; *cf. n.*   120. 8 weigh: *consider*
9, 10 *Cf. n.*   11 then tender'd: *then had I tendered*
13 fee: *payment, recompense*

121

'Tis better to be vile than vile esteem'd,
When not to be receives reproach of being;
And the just pleasure lost, which is so deem'd
Not by our feeling, but by others' seeing: 4
For why should others' false adulterate eyes
Give salutation to my sportive blood?
Or on my frailties why are frailer spies,
Which in their wills count bad what I think good? 8
No, I am that I am, and they that level
At my abuses reckon up their own:
I may be straight though they themselves be bevel;
By their rank thoughts my deeds must not be shown; 12
   Unless this general evil they maintain,
    All men are bad and in their badness reign.

122

Thy gift, thy tables, are within my brain
Full character'd with lasting memory,
Which shall above that idle rank remain,
Beyond all date, even to eternity: 4
Or, at the least, so long as brain and heart
Have faculty by nature to subsist;
Till each to raz'd oblivion yield his part
Of thee, thy record never can be miss'd. 8
That poor retention could not so much hold,
Nor need I tallies thy dear love to score;
Therefore to give them from me was I bold,
To trust those tables that receive thee more: 12
   To keep an adjunct to remember thee
    Were to import forgetfulness in me.

3, 4 *Cf. n.*
6 Give salutation to: *greet (as if Shakespeare were one of them)*
  sportive: *wanton*   3 in their wills: *as they please*   11 bevel: *oblique*
1-14 *Cf. n.*   1 tables: *memorandum book*
3 idle rank: *empty row of leaves*   7 raz'd: *empty*
9 poor retention: *book that contains little* 10 tallies . . . score; *cf. n.*
12 those tables: *my memory*   13 adjunct: *attendant*

123

No, Time, thou shalt not boast that I do change:
Thy pyramids built up with newer might
To me are nothing novel, nothing strange;
They are but dressings of a former sight.   **4**
Our dates are brief, and therefore we admire
What thou dost foist upon us that is old;
And rather make them born to our desire
Than think that we before have heard them told.   **8**
Thy registers and thee I both defy,
Not wondering at the present nor the past,
For thy records and what we see doth lie,
Made more or less by thy continual haste.   **12**

    This I do vow, and this shall ever be;
    I will be true, despite thy scythe and thee.

124

If my dear love were but the child of state,
It might for Fortune's bastard be unfather'd,
As subject to Time's love or to Time's hate,
Weeds among weeds, or flowers with flowers gather'd. **4**
No, it was builded far from accident;
It suffers not in smiling pomp, nor falls
Under the blow of thralled discontent,
Whereto the inviting time our fashion calls: **8**
It fears not policy, that heretic,
Which works on leases of short number'd hours,
But all alone stands hugely politic,
That it nor grows with heat, nor drowns with showers.

    To this I witness call the fools of time,   **13**
    Which die for goodness, who have liv'd for crime.

2 newer: *more recent*   4 dressings: *refashionings*
5 dates: *years of life*   7, 8 *Cf. n.*   11 doth lie: *doth tell us a lie*
12 Made more or less: *increasing and decreasing, constantly changing*
1 child of state: *born of circumstances, accidental*
2 for: *because it was*   4 Weeds . . . gather'd; *cf. n.*
7 thralled discontent: *discontent held in subjection*
8 Whereto: *to which*   fashion: *custom, usage*
9 policy: *craft*   11 hugely politic: *extremely wise*   13, 14 *Cf. n.*

125

Were 't aught to me I bore the canopy,
With my extern the outward honouring,
Or laid great bases for eternity,
Which prove more short than waste or ruining?   4
Have I not seen dwellers on form and favour
Lose all and more by paying too much rent,
For compound sweet forgoing simple savour,
Pitiful thrivers, in their gazing spent?   8
No; let me be obsequious in thy heart,
And take thou my oblation, poor but free,
Which is not mix'd with seconds, knows no art,
But mutual render, only me for thee.   12
  Hence, thou suborn'd informer! a true soul
  When most impeach'd stands least in thy control.

126

O thou, my lovely boy, who in thy power
Dost hold Time's fickle glass, his sickle hour;
Who hast by waning grown, and therein show'st
Thy lovers withering as thy sweet self grow'st;   4
If Nature, sovereign mistress over wrack,
As thou goest onwards, still will pluck thee back,
She keeps thee to this purpose, that her skill
May time disgrace and wretched minutes kill.   8
Yet fear her, O thou minion of her pleasure!
She may detain, but not still keep, her treasure:
  Her audit, though delay'd, answer'd must be,
  And her quietus is to render thee.   12

1 Were 't: *would it be*   bore the canopy: *canopy of state; did outward reverence*   2 With my extern: *outwardly*
7 savour: *perfume*
8 in their gazing spent: *wasting themselves in regarding externals*
10 free: *whole-hearted*   11 seconds: *inferior matter*
12 render: *surrender*   13, 14 *Cf. n.*   1-12 *Cf. n.*
2 sickle hour: *hour when his sickle strikes*
3 by waning grown: *with age grown more beautiful*
5 wrack: *destruction*
8 wretched minutes kill: *kill time's minutes (that bring old age)*
9 minion: *darling*   12 quietus: *acquittance of the account*

127

In the old age black was not counted fair,
Or if it were, it bore not beauty's name;
But now is black beauty's successive heir,
And beauty slander'd with a bastard's shame: 4
For since each hand hath put on Nature's power,
Fairing the foul with Art's false borrow'd face,
Sweet beauty hath no name, no holy bower,
But is profan'd, if not lives in disgrace.   8
Therefore my mistress' brows are raven black,
Her eyes so suited, and they mourners seem
At such who, not born fair, no beauty lack,
Sland'ring creation with a false esteem: 12
   Yet so they mourn, becoming of their woe,
   That every tongue says beauty should look so.

128

How oft, when thou, my music, music play'st,
Upon that blessed wood whose motion sounds
With thy sweet fingers, when thou gently sway'st
The wiry concord that mine ear confounds,   4
Do I envy those jacks that nimble leap
To kiss the tender inward of thy hand,
Whilst my poor lips, which should that harvest reap,
At the wood's boldness by thee blushing stand!   8
To be so tickl'd, they would change their state
And situation with those dancing chips,
O'er whom thy fingers walk with gentle gait,
Making dead wood more bless'd than living lips.   12
   Since saucy jacks so happy are in this,
   Give them thy fingers, me thy lips to kiss.

1-14 *Cf. n.*   1 black . . . fair; *cf. n.*   3 successive: *legitimate*
6 Fairing . . . face: *beautifying ugliness by cosmetics*
10 suited: *attired*
11 no beauty lack: *make themselves beautiful by artifice*
13 so: *in such a manner*   becoming of: *gracing*
4 wiry concord: *harmony of the wires*   5 jacks; *cf. n.*

129

The expense of spirit in a waste of shame
Is lust in action; and till action, lust
Is perjur'd, murderous, bloody, full of blame,
Savage, extreme, rude, cruel, not to trust;　　　4
Enjoy'd no sooner but despised straight;
Past reason hunted; and no sooner had,
Past reason hated, as a swallow'd bait,
On purpose laid to make the taker mad:　　　8
Mad in pursuit, and in possession so;
Had, having, and in quest to have, extreme;
A bliss in proof, and prov'd, a very woe;
Before, a joy propos'd; behind, a dream.　　　12
　　All this the world well knows; yet none knows well
　　To shun the heaven that leads men to this hell.

130

My mistress' eyes are nothing like the sun;
Coral is far more red than her lips' red:
If snow be white, why then her breasts are dun;
If hairs be wires, black wires grow on her head.　　　4
I have seen roses damask'd, red and white,
But no such roses see I in her cheeks;
And in some perfumes is there more delight
Than in the breath that from my mistress reeks.　　　8
I love to hear her speak, yet well I know
That music hath a far more pleasing sound:
I grant I never saw a goddess go;
My mistress, when she walks, treads on the ground: 12
　　And yet, by heaven, I think my love as rare
　　As any she belied with false compare.

1-3 *Cf. n.*　　　4 extreme: *violent*　　　6 Past: *beyond all*
11 in proof: *when experienced*　　　12 propos'd: *anticipated*
5 damask'd: *of the shade of a damask rose*
14 compare: *comparisons*

131

Thou art as tyrannous, so as thou art,
As those whose beauties proudly make them cruel;
For well thou know'st to my dear doting heart
Thou art the fairest and most precious jewel.   4
Yet, in good faith, some say that thee behold,
Thy face hath not the power to make love groan:
To say they err I dare not be so bold,
Although I swear it to myself alone.   8
And to be sure that is not false I swear,
A thousand groans, but thinking on thy face,
One on another's neck, do witness bear
Thy black is fairest in my judgment's place.   12

   In nothing art thou black save in thy deeds,
   And thence this slander, as I think, proceeds.

132

Thine eyes I love, and they, as pitying me,
Knowing thy heart torments me with disdain,
Have put on black and loving mourners be,
Looking with pretty ruth upon my pain.   4
And truly not the morning sun of heaven
Better becomes the grey cheeks of the east,
Nor that full star that ushers in the even,
Doth half that glory to the sober west,   8
As those two mourning eyes become thy face:
O, let it then as well beseem thy heart
To mourn for me, since mourning doth thee grace,
And suit thy pity like in every part.   12

   Then will I swear beauty herself is black,
   And all they foul that thy complexion lack.

---

1 so as: *homely as*   10 but: *only on*
11 One . . . neck: *in quick succession*   4 ruth: *pity*
12 suit: *attire*   like: *alike*   14 foul: *ugly*

133

Beshrew that heart that makes my heart to groan
For that deep wound it gives my friend and me!
Is 't not enough to torture me alone,
But slave to slavery my sweet'st friend must be?   4
Me from myself thy cruel eye hath taken,
And my next self thou harder hast engross'd:
Of him, myself, and thee, I am forsaken;
A torment thrice threefold thus to be cross'd.   8
Prison my heart in thy steel bosom's ward,
But then my friend's heart let my poor heart bail;
Whoe'er keeps me, let my heart be his guard;
Thou canst not then use rigour in my jail: 12
    And yet thou wilt; for I, being pent in thee,
    Perforce am thine, and all that is in me.

134

So, now I have confess'd that he is thine,
And I myself am mortgag'd to thy will,
Myself I'll forfeit, so that other mine
Thou wilt restore, to be my comfort still: 4
But thou wilt not, nor he will not be free,
For thou art covetous and he is kind;
He learn'd but surety-like to write for me,
Under that bond that him as fast doth bind.   8
The statute of thy beauty thou wilt take,
Thou usurer, that putt'st forth all to use,
And sue a friend came debtor for my sake;
So him I lose through my unkind abuse.   12
    Him have I lost; thou hast both him and me:
    He pays the whole, and yet am I not free.

6 my next self: *my friend*   engross'd: *gained exclusive possession of*
10 bail: *go bail for (?), guard (?)*   3 other mine: *other self*
5 nor he will not be free: *nor does he wish freedom*
7 He learn'd . . . me: *he released me by pledging himself as security*
9 statute of thy beauty: *bond giving possession obtained by thy beauty*
10 to use: *to interest*   11 came: *who became*
12 my unkind abuse: *unnatural wrong done to me*

135

Whoever hath her wish, thou hast thy *Will*,
And *Will* to boot, and *Will* in over-plus;
More than enough am I that vex thee still,
To thy sweet will making addition thus.   4
Wilt thou, whose will is large and spacious,
Not once vouchsafe to hide my will in thine?
Shall will in others seem right gracious,
And in my will no fair acceptance shine?   8
The sea, all water, yet receives rain still,
And in abundance addeth to his store;
So thou, being rich in *Will*, add to thy *Will*
One will of mine, to make thy large *Will* more.   12
    Let no unkind 'No' fair beseechers kill;
      Think all but one, and me in that one *Will*.

136

If thy soul check thee that I come so near,
Swear to thy blind soul that I was thy *Will*,
And will, thy soul knows, is admitted there;
Thus far for love my love-suit, sweet, fulfil.   4
Will will fulfil the treasure of thy love,
Ay, fill it full with wills, and my will one.
In things of great receipt with ease we prove
Among a number one is reckon'd none: 8
Then in the number let me pass untold,
Though in thy stores' account I one must be;
For nothing hold me, so it please thee hold
That nothing me, a something sweet to thee: 12
    Make but my name thy love, and love that still,
      And then thou lov'st me,—for my name is *Will*.

1-14 *Cf. n.*
7 receipt: *capacity*

136. 1 check: *reprove*
9 untold: *uncounted*

137

Thou blind fool, Love, what dost thou to mine eyes,
That they behold, and see not what they see?
They know what beauty is, see where it lies,
Yet what the best is take the worst to be.　　4
If eyes, corrupt by over-partial looks,
Be anchor'd in the bay where all men ride,
Why of eyes' falsehood hast thou forged hooks,
Whereto the judgment of my heart is tied?　　8
Why should my heart think that a several plot
Which my heart knows the wide world's common
　　place?
Or mine eyes, seeing this, say this is not,
To put fair truth upon so foul a face?　　12
　　In things right true my heart and eyes have err'd,
　　And to this false plague are they now transferr'd.

138

When my love swears that she is made of truth,
I do believe her, though I know she lies,
That she might think me some untutor'd youth,
Unlearned in the world's false subtleties.　　4
Thus vainly thinking that she thinks me young,
Although she knows my days are past the best,
Simply I credit her false-speaking tongue:
On both sides thus is simple truth supprest.　　8
But wherefore says she not she is unjust?
And wherefore say not I that I am old?
O, love's best habit is in seeming trust,
And age in love loves not to have years told:　　12
　　Therefore I lie with her, and she with me,
　　And in our faults by lies we flatter'd be.

9 several: *private*
7 Simply: *absolutely*

1-14 *Cf. n.*
9 unjust: *false*

139

O, call not me to justify the wrong
That thy unkindness lays upon my heart;
Wound me not with thine eye, but with thy tongue:
Use power with power, and slay me not by art.   4
Tell me thou lov'st elsewhere; but in my sight,
Dear heart, forbear to glance thine eye aside:
What need'st thou wound with cunning, when thy
      might
Is more than my o'erpress'd defence can bide?   8
Let me excuse thee: ah! my love well knows
Her pretty looks have been my enemies;
And therefore from my face she turns my foes,
That they elsewhere might dart their injuries: 12
      Yet do not so; but since I am near slain,
      Kill me outright with looks, and rid my pain.

140

Be wise as thou art cruel; do not press
My tongue-tied patience with too much disdain;
Lest sorrow lend me words, and words express
The manner of my pity-wanting pain.   4
If I might teach thee wit, better it were,
Though not to love, yet, love, to tell me so;
As testy sick men, when their deaths be near,
No news but health from their physicians know;   8
For, if I should despair, I should grow mad,
And in my madness might speak ill of thee:
Now this ill-wresting world is grown so bad,
Mad slanderers by mad ears believed be.   12
      That I may not be so, nor thou belied,
      Bear thine eyes straight, though thy proud heart go
      wide.

4 by art: *by cunning*   140. 4 pity-wanting pain: *unpitied suffering*
11 ill-wresting: *maliciously misconstruing*

141

In faith, I do not love thee with mine eyes,
For they in thee a thousand errors note;
But 'tis my heart that loves what they despise,
Who, in despite of view, is pleas'd to dote. 4
Nor are mine ears with thy tongue's tune delighted;
Nor tender feeling to base touches prone.
Nor taste nor smell desire to be invited
To any sensual feast with thee alone: 8
But my five wits nor my five senses can
Dissuade one foolish heart from serving thee,
Who leaves unsway'd the likeness of a man,
Thy proud heart's slave and vassal wretch to be: 12
    Only my plague thus far I count my gain,
    That she that makes me sin awards me pain.

142

Love is my sin, and thy dear virtue hate,
Hate of my sin, grounded on sinful loving:
O, but with mine compare thou thine own state,
And thou shalt find it merits not reproving; 4
Or, if it do, not from those lips of thine,
That have profan'd their scarlet ornaments
And seal'd false bonds of love as oft as mine,
Robb'd others' beds' revenues of their rents. 8
Be it lawful I love thee, as thou lov'st those
Whom thine eyes woo as mine importune thee:
Root pity in thy heart, that when it grows,
Thy pity may deserve to pitied be. 12
    If thou dost seek to have what thou dost hide,
    By self-example mayst thou be denied!

9 five wits; *cf. n.*   **11** unsway'd: *deprived of self-control* (?)
14 pain: *punishment*   **13** what thou dost hide: *the love you refuse*

143

Lo, as a careful housewife runs to catch
One of her feather'd creatures broke away,
Sets down her babe, and makes all quick dispatch
In pursuit of the thing she would have stay;　　4
Whilst her neglected child holds her in chase,
Cries to catch her whose busy care is bent
To follow that which flies before her face,
Not prizing her poor infant's discontent:　　8
So runn'st thou after that which flies from thee,
Whilst I thy babe chase thee afar behind;
But if thou catch thy hope, turn back to me,
And play the mother's part, kiss me, be kind;　　12
　　So will I pray that thou mayst have thy *Will,*
　　If thou turn back and my loud crying still.

144

Two loves I have of comfort and despair,
Which like two spirits do suggest me still:
The better angel is a man right fair,
The worser spirit a woman, colour'd ill.　　4
To win me soon to hell, my female evil
Tempteth my better angel from my side,
And would corrupt my saint to be a devil,
Wooing his purity with her foul pride.　　8
And whether that my angel be turn'd fiend
Suspect I may, but not directly tell;
But being both from me, both to each friend,
I guess one angel in another's hell:　　12
　　Yet this shall I ne'er know, but live in doubt,
　　Till my bad angel fire my good one out.

13 Will; *cf. note on Sonnet 135*　　　　　1-14 *Cf. n.*
2 suggest: *prompt*
11 from me: *away from me*　　　to each: *to each other*
14 fire . . . out: *drive out with fire*

145

Those lips that Love's own hand did make,
Breath'd forth the sound that said 'I hate,'
To me that languish'd for her sake:
But when she saw my woeful state, 4
Straight in her heart did mercy come,
Chiding that tongue that ever sweet
Was us'd in giving gentle doom;
And taught it thus anew to greet; 8
'I hate,' she alter'd with an end,
That follow'd it as gentle day
Doth follow night, who like a fiend
From heaven to hell is flown away. 12
   'I hate' from hate away she threw,
    And sav'd my life, saying—'Not you.'

146

Poor soul, the centre of my sinful earth,
Fool'd by these rebel powers that thee array,
Why dost thou pine within and suffer dearth,
Painting thy outward walls so costly gay? 4
Why so large cost, having so short a lease,
Dost thou upon thy fading mansion spend?
Shall worms, inheritors of this excess,
Eat up thy charge? Is this thy body's end? 8
Then, soul, live thou upon thy servant's loss,
And let that pine to aggravate thy store;
Buy terms divine in selling hours of dross;
Within be fed, without be rich no more: 12
   So shalt thou feed on Death, that feeds on men,
    And Death once dead, there's no more dying then.

1-14 *Cf. n.*   146. 1, 2 *Cf. n.*   4 outward walls: *body*
8 charge: *expense*   10 aggravate: *increase*
11 terms: *long periods of time*

147

My love is as a fever, longing still
For that which longer nurseth the disease;
Feeding on that which doth preserve the ill,
The uncertain sickly appetite to please.   4
My reason, the physician to my love,
Angry that his prescriptions are not kept,
Hath left me, and I desperate now approve
Desire is death, which physic did except.   8
Past cure I am, now reason is past care,
And frantic-mad with evermore unrest;
My thoughts and my discourse as madmen's are,
At random from the truth vainly express'd;   12

    For I have sworn thee fair, and thought thee bright,
    Who art as black as hell, as dark as night.

148

O me! what eyes hath Love put in my head,
Which have no correspondence with true sight;
Or, if they have, where is my judgment fled,
That censures falsely what they see aright?   4
If that be fair whereon my false eyes dote,
What means the world to say it is not so?
If it be not, then love doth well denote
Love's eye is not so true as all men's: no.   8
How can it? O, how can Love's eye be true,
That is so vex'd with watching and with tears?
No marvel then, though I mistake my view;
The sun itself sees not till heaven clears.   12

    O cunning Love! with tears thou keep'st me blind,
    Lest eyes well-seeing thy foul faults should find.

6 kept: *followed*   7 approve: *prove that*
8 which physic did except: (*Desire*) *which objected to the physic (of Reason*)   4 censures: *judges*   10 watching: *wakefulness*

149

Canst thou, O cruel! say I love thee not,
When I against myself with thee partake?
Do I not think on thee, when I forgot
Am of myself, all tyrant, for thy sake?   4
Who hateth thee that I do call my friend?
On whom frown'st thou that I do fawn upon?
Nay, if thou lour'st on me, do I not spend
Revenge upon myself with present moan?   8
What merit do I in myself respect,
That is so proud thy service to despise,
When all my best doth worship thy defect,
Commanded by the motion of thine eyes?   12
    But, love, hate on, for now I know thy mind;
    Those that can see thou lov'st, and I am blind.

150

O, from what power hast thou this powerful might,
With insufficiency my heart to sway?
To make me give the lie to my true sight,
And swear that brightness doth not grace the day?   4
Whence hast thou this becoming of things ill,
That in the very refuse of thy deeds
There is such strength and warrantise of skill,
That, in my mind, thy worst all best exceeds?   8
Who taught thee how to make me love thee more,
The more I hear and see just cause of hate?
O, though I love what others do abhor,
With others thou shouldst not abhor my state: 12
    If thy unworthiness rais'd love in me,
    More worthy I to be belov'd of thee.

2 with thee partake: *take part with thee*
4 all tyrant: *you absolute tyrant*
7 warrantise: *assurance*

9 respect: *prize*

151

Love is too young to know what conscience is;
Yet who knows not conscience is born of love?
Then, gentle cheater, urge not my amiss,
Lest guilty of my faults thy sweet self prove: 4
For, thou betraying me, I do betray
My nobler part to my gross body's treason;
My soul doth tell my body that he may
Triumph in love; flesh stays no further reason,   8
But rising at thy name doth point out thee
As his triumphant prize.   Proud of this pride,
He is contented thy poor drudge to be,
To stand in thy affairs, fall by thy side.   12
     No want of conscience hold it that I call
     Her 'love' for whose dear love I rise and fall.

152

In loving thee thou know'st I am forsworn,
But thou art twice forsworn, to me love swearing;
In act thy bed-vow broke, and new faith torn,
In vowing new hate after new love bearing.   4
But why of two oaths' breach do I accuse thee,
When I break twenty?   I am perjur'd most;
For all my vows are oaths but to misuse thee,
And all my honest faith in thee is lost: 8
For I have sworn deep oaths of thy deep kindness,
Oaths of thy love, thy truth, thy constancy;
And, to enlighten thee, gave eyes to blindness,
Or made them swear against the thing they see;   12
     For I have sworn thee fair; more perjur'd I,
     To swear against the truth so foul a lie!

152. 3 torn: *broken*   7 misuse: *speak falsely of*
11 enlighten: *shed lustre upon*

153

Cupid laid by his brand and fell asleep:
A maid of Dian's this advantage found,
And his love-kindling fire did quickly steep
In a cold valley-fountain of that ground; 4
Which borrow'd from this holy fire of Love
A dateless lively heat, still to endure,
And grew a seething bath, which yet men prove
Against strange maladies a sovereign cure. 8
But at my mistress' eye Love's brand new-fired,
The boy for trial needs would touch my breast;
I, sick withal, the help of bath desired,
And thither hied, a sad distemper'd guest, 12
   But found no cure: the bath for my help lies
   Where Cupid got new fire, my mistress' eyes.

154

The little Love-god lying once asleep
Laid by his side his heart-inflaming brand,
Whilst many nymphs that vow'd chaste life to keep
Came tripping by; but in her maiden hand 4
The fairest votary took up that fire
Which many legions of true hearts had warm'd;
And so the general of hot desire
Was, sleeping, by a virgin hand disarm'd. 8
This brand she quenched in a cool well by,
Which from Love's fire took heat perpetual,
Growing a bath and healthful remedy
For men diseas'd; but I, my mistress' thrall, 12
   Came there for cure, and this by that I prove,
   Love's fire heats water, water cools not love.

1-14 *Cf. n.*   1 brand: *torch*   2 advantage: *favorable opportunity*
6 dateless: *eternal*   9 new-fired: *kindled again*
1-14 *Cf. n.*   13 this: *this truth: Love's fire, etc.*

FINIS.

NOTES

Dedication

1. *onlie begetter.* Some scholars, notably Lee, argue that 'begetter' here means 'obtainer,' 'procurer'; hence the publisher T. T. is thanking W. H. for finding and delivering to him the MSS. of this sonnet collection. Lee goes further and identifies W. H. as William Hall, a stationer of the period. Mrs. Stopes, practically following Lee's interpretation of 'begetter,' identifies W. H. as William Harvey, the stepfather of the third Earl of Southampton, Shakespeare's friend. The natural rendering of this phrase which recalls the 'only begotten' of the Creed, is 'the one, the only, inspirer.'

3. *W. H.* These initials raise a controversy which many volumes have not yet settled. If we reject Lee's interpretation and believe that a nobleman must be the inspirer of the sonnets praising a youth, the two best candidates are William Herbert, third Earl of Pembroke, and Henry Wriothesley (pronounced 'Rizley'), third Earl of Southampton. Of the two, Southampton seems the better claimant, though Herbert's liaison with Mary Fitton and her subsequent career has led many (especially dramatists) to consider her the heroine of the last group of sonnets. But Herbert came to court as late as 1598 and the sonnets, as a whole, seem to have been written before that year. Southampton is the only patron Shakespeare publicly acknowledged, and the dedication of *Venus and Adonis,* 1593, and *The Rape of Lucrece,* 1594, show that the poet regarded him with gratitude and affection. If, as seems more probable, W. H. was not a great nobleman, other names have been suggested: William Hall, William Harvey (*vide supra*), William

Hughes, William Hammond, William Hathaway. It is perfectly evident that Shakespeare must have had many friends whose very names, to say nothing of initials, Time has effaced. All that can be said with certainty of the hero of these sonnets is that he was a youth of better birth and fortune than Shakespeare and that his encouragement and friendship, at a certain period in the poet's career, won Shakespeare's praise and devotion. In his gratitude, Shakespeare, as he said, built in these sonnets an enduring monument; unfortunately for us T. T. wrote its inscription. The best short account of this whole controversy is found in Alden's variorum edition of the sonnets, pp. 464-471, prepared by Frank E. Hill.

13. *T. T.* Thomas Thorpe. Lee describes him as a stationer's assistant, 'holding his own with difficulty for some thirty years in the lowest ranks of the London publishing trade. He merely traded in the "copy" which he procured how he could.' See also R. B. McKerrow, *Dictionary of Printers and Booksellers,* p. 265 f.

SONNETS

1. These first seventeen sonnets are addressed to a beautiful youth whose identity is still a subject of conjecture. They urge him by flattery, expostulation, and argument to marry and perpetuate his beauty in a child.

1. 6. *Feed'st thy light's flame with self-substantial fuel.* Like a candle, you feed your flame by burning your own substance; or, you feed your eyes (light's flame) on the sight of yourself—you see only yourself.

1. 11. *content.* In this line, this word may also mean 'your whole being.'

1. 13, 14. *Pity the world, or else this glutton be, To eat the world's due, by the grave and thee.* This may

be paraphrased: Pity the world (by perpetuating your beauty in your children) or glutton-like, you eat your beauty, due the world, by allowing it to perish in the grave and by your failure to beget children.

5. 9, 10. A reference to perfumes extracted from flowers. Compare the close of sonnet 54.

7. 9-12. *But when from highmost pitch, with weary car, Like feeble age, he reeleth from the day, The eyes, 'fore duteous, now converted are From his low tract, and look another way.* Cf. 'All this blanked not Pompey, who told him frankly againe, how men did honour the rising, not the setting of the sunne; meaning thereby, how his owne honor encreased, and Scyllaes diminished.' *Life of Pompey* in *Plutarch's Lives of the Noble Grecians and Romans englished by Sir Thomas North* (1579).

8. 14. *'Thou single wilt prove none.'* 'Perhaps an allusion to the proverbial expression that one is no number.' Dowden. Compare sonnet 136, line 8.

11. 11. *Look, whom she best endow'd she gave the more.* See, to you whom Nature best endowed she gives an added gift.

13. 1. *O that you were yourself.* O that you were yourself forever.

14. 12. *If from thyself to store thou wouldst convert.* If you would turn from living for yourself alone and would beget children.

15. 4. *secret influence.* Astrology taught that there emanated from the stars a power or force (secret influence) which determined the characters and the fortunes of men and states.

16. 10. *Which this Time's pencil, or my pupil pen.* Beeching gives the following paraphrase: 'Neither portraiture ("this Time's pencil," cf. line 8) nor description ("my pupil pen," cf. line 4) can represent you as you are, either in character or beauty.'

18. Sonnets 18-25 form a single series, praising the

youth's beauty and declaring the poet's affection for him.

19. 10. *antique pen.* This word, pronounced 'antic,' may mean in this sonnet not merely 'old' (cf. sonnet 106. 7) but also 'a pen that plays pranks, that draws grotesque lines.'

20. This sonnet has hardly the tone in which Shakespeare, the actor, could address a nobleman of high rank.

20. 7. *A man in hue all hues in his controlling.* This line is a source of perpetual debate. The Quarto prints 'all *Hews*,' and some editors have seen here a pun on the name Hughes, even suggesting that this proves 'W. H.' to have been William Hughes. Other editors change the reading 'A man in hue' to 'A native hue' or 'A maiden hue.' Shakespeare has just said that his friend has a woman's gentle heart, an eye that is brighter than a woman's, and in this line, going a step further, he gives to him a man's complexion of such beauty that it overpowers or surpasses the handsome coloring of all others.

24. 4. *perspective.* An optical instrument for viewing objects, a magnifying glass. Notice the pun in the next line, 'through the painter.' Shakespeare is also alluding to the more familiar meaning of perspective. The N. E. D. cites Haydocke, 1598, 'A painter without the perspective was like a doctor without grammar.'

26. By some editors, this sonnet is regarded as an envoi to the preceding twenty-five sonnets. 'This written ambassage' (line 3) may refer to that series; but it may equally well refer to this sonnet only.

34. 13, 14. *Ah! but those tears are pearl which thy love sheds, And they are rich and ransom all ill deeds.* Cf. *Antony and Cleopatra,* III. ix. 69-71.

> Fall not a tear, I say; one of them rates
> All that is won and lost. Give me a kiss;
> Even this repays me.

This and the following sonnet may refer to the incident described in sonnets 40-42.

35. 8. *Excusing thy sins more than thy sins are.* Not only the meaning of this line but the correctness of the text itself is a debated question. Q. reads 'their' for 'thy' in both instances; Bullen reads: 'Excusing their sins more than thy sins are.' The present reading is the one most generally adopted. This line and the preceding one may be paraphrased: I am corrupting myself in condoning your fault, for I am so anxious to exculpate you that I offer for you excuses out of all proportion to your sins.

35. 9. *sense.* Not 'reason' but rather 'the senses, the feelings.' The poet's own feelings urge him to excuse the guilt of his friend.

36. 13, 14. *But do not so; I love thee in such sort As thou being mine, mine is thy good report.* But do not dishonor yourself (by showing me kindness in the eyes of the world), for my love has so completely taken possession of you that your good name, your honor, belongs to me. (Note that this same couplet occurs at the close of sonnet 96.)

37. 5-7. Apparently the youth Shakespeare praises is better born, richer, and handsomer than the poet; yet these lines do not prove him to be one of the nobility.

39. 13, 14. *And that thou teachest how to make one twain, By praising him here who doth hence remain.* This may be paraphrased: And because, Absence, you teach me to make of one person two—my friend is away from me and yet I may call him before my memory and seem while praising him to enjoy his presence.

40. There is nothing to prove that the woman of sonnets 40-42 is the 'dark' woman of sonnets 127 ff.

40. 8. *By wilful taste of what thyself refusest.* Dowden paraphrases this: 'By an unlawful union

while you refuse loyal wedlock'; Beeching conjec-
tures: 'By taking in wilfulness my mistress whom yet
you do not love.'

44. 14. *badges of either's woe.* The poet's heavy
tears are the signs of woe of the two elements in his
body, earth and water. In the first line of the next
sonnet, Shakespeare alludes to the two remaining elements, fire and air. According to the belief of Shakespeare's day, man was composed of these four elements.

51. 11. *Shall neigh—no dull flesh—in his fiery
race.* It is possible that the text of this obscure line is
corrupt. As it stands, the thought may be expressed
as follows: (Desire), no dull, plodding beast, shall
neigh like a spirited horse as it rushes on its fiery race
to you.

58. 6. *The imprison'd absence of your liberty.*
Beeching paraphrases this: 'suffer your absence,
which, though it represent liberty to you, means im-
prisonment to me.'

60. 4. *In sequent toil all forwards do contend.*
Toiling and following each other all (the waves) strive
onward.

62. 10. This line and the opening lines of the following sonnet give no definite information whatever
concerning Shakespeare's age when he wrote these
poems. It was a common convention of both English
and Continental sonneteers to contrast their wrinkled
faces and advanced years with the lovely youth of the
person they were praising.

67. 7, 8. *Why should poor beauty indirectly seek
Roses of shadow.* In this line 'indirectly' means 'dis-
honestly.' Shakespeare is inveighing against the
fashionable practice of rouging or painting the face.
This protest was a common one; it was expressed in
many moods, including Hamlet's passionate outburst
(*Hamlet* III. i. 150 ff.).

68. 3. Here the poet attacks the fashionable prac-

tice of wearing wigs. According to Stow, the custom of wearing them began in England in 1572.

69. 14. *soil.* The N. E. D. explains the word in this line as 'The solution of the problem.'

70. If this sonnet is addressed to the youth of sonnets 34-35, 40-42, it is plainly out of place, for here the youth's life is pronounced blameless.

71. 2, 3. This alludes to the custom of tolling the church bell when a member of the parish died, one stroke for each year of the deceased.

73. 12. *Consum'd with that which it was nourish'd by.* The wood which fed the fire is now turned to ashes and extinguishes the flame.

77. Apparently this sonnet was either written in a blank book sent to the unknown friend, or else it accompanied such a gift. It is out of place between sonnets 76 and 78 which discuss Shakespeare's own writings.

77. 4. *And of this book this learning mayst thou taste.* Dowden makes the following comment: 'Beauty, Time, and Verse formed the theme of many of Shakespeare's sonnets; now that he will write no more, he commends his friend to his glass, where he may discover the truth about his beauty; to the dial, where he may learn the progress of time; and to this book, which he himself—not Shakespeare—must fill.'

77. 11, 12. *Those children nurs'd, deliver'd from thy brain, To take a new acquaintance of thy mind.* The meaning of these lines may be expressed: Your thoughts, written in the pages ('waste blanks') of this book, will seem new when you reread them, as children, sent out to nurse, are grown and changed when brought back to their parents.

77. 13. *These offices.* The habitual use, in the manner suggested by the poet, of the dial and mirror.

78. This begins a series of nine sonnets in which Shakespeare laments that his friend has turned from

Shakespeare's verses to the poetry of a 'better spirit.'
Cf. the next note.

80. 2. *Knowing a better spirit doth use your name.*
No one has yet established the identity of this 'better
spirit' who supplanted Shakespeare in the esteem of
his friend and to whom in this sonnet and in the ones
immediately following, Shakespeare acknowledges
himself far inferior. Attempts have been made to
show that the rival poet was Barnes, Chapman, Daniel,
Drayton, Jonson, Marston; yet nothing has been
proved.

83. 14. *Than both your poets can in praise devise.*
That one of these poets must be Shakespeare is quite
evident.

84. 3, 4. *In whose confine immured is the store
Which should example where your equal grew?* You,
in whom is stored up the whole sum of your unex-
ampled beauty.

84. 14. *Being fond on praise, which makes your
praises worse.* Being fond of receiving praise which,
as it never does you justice, really detracts from you
(makes your praises worse).

85. 3. *Reserve their character with golden quill.*
This may be paraphrased: (The comments of your
praise, l. 2) are written down in a form that will
endure (reserve their character), in a beautiful style
(with golden quill).

85. 7. *able spirit.* Another reference to the rival
poet whose 'hymns' have proved as elusive as his name.

85. 12. *Though words come hindmost, holds his
rank before.* This, and the preceding line, may be
expressed as follows: Though my words are not equal
to your praises sung by another, the loving praise in
my mind outranks the tributes of everyone.

87. 3. *The charter of thy worth gives thee releasing.*
You do not belong to me because your fine qualities
give you the privilege of leaving me.

90. 6.   *Come in the rearward of a conquer'd woe.*
Attack me after I have defeated one misfortune.

94.   It is interesting to compare this sonnet on self-
control with Hamlet's famous praise of the man who
is not passion's slave (*Hamlet* III. ii. 59-79).

94. 9-12.   Wyndham paraphrases these lines: 'These
self-contained persons may seem to lack generosity;
but then, without making voluntary gifts, they give
inevitably, even as the summer's flower is sweet to the
summer, though it live and die only to itself.   Yet let
such one beware of corruption.'

94. 14.   This line occurs in the anonymous play of
Edward III (published in 1596), II. i. 51.   Though
the opinion is not unanimous, many Shakespearean
scholars believe the sonnet antedates the play, to which
Shakespeare has sometimes been thought to have con-
tributed certain scenes.

96. 13, 14.   This couplet concludes sonnet 36 where,
as many critics observe, it is more in keeping with the
general idea of the poem.

99. 7.   *buds of marjoram.*   The reference may be
either to the color of the buds—reddish brown—or to
their fragrance.

107. 1-4.   The first four lines of this sonnet may be
paraphrased: Neither my own fears, nor the divining
soul of the world dreaming of the future to which the
present shall give way, can overpower the duration of
my love, mistakenly supposed to be subject to the fate
that limits all things.

107. 5.   *mortal moon.*   Many scholars find in this
sonnet definite allusions to contemporary events.   Lee
and others believe it celebrates the release of Southampton from prison, 1603.   He was set free after the
death of Elizabeth, whom contemporary poets cele-
brated as the moon goddess.   ('The mortal moon hath
her eclipse endured.')   The motto of James I, who
released Southampton, was 'Blessed are the peace-

makers' (cf. l. 8). To others, the sonnet celebrates the defeat of the Armada, or the reconciliation of Elizabeth with Essex. It is equally possible to read this sonnet as merely one more in the series in which Shakespeare proclaims his devotion to be superior to fate and death.

108. 13, 14. *Finding the first conceit of love there bred, Where time and outward form would show it dead.* Finding the first love still inspired in a face whose appearance of age would make it unlovely to others.

110. 1, 2. These lines refer, probably, though not necessarily, to Shakespeare's career as an actor. They lament, as do the following two sonnets, the associations forced upon him by poverty.

112. 7, 8. *None else to me, nor I to none alive, That my steel'd sense or changes right or wrong.* So far as I am concerned, no one but you (and I live for you alone) can influence my callous feeling to right or wrong.

112. 10, 11. *that my adder's sense To critic and to flatterer stopped are.* This may be a reminiscence of Psalm 58. 4, 5: 'Even like the deaf adder, that stoppeth her ears; Which refuseth to hear the voice of the charmer, charm he never so wisely.'

113. 14. *My most true mind thus maketh mine untrue.* Malone explains this line: 'The sincerity of my affection is the cause of my untruth; i.e., of not seeing objects truly, such as they appear to the rest of mankind.'

114. 13, 14. In line 12, the eye has been compared to the taster for king Mind. If the eye gives him a poisoned cup, it is not such a great sin because the eye drinks the poison first.

119. 7. *How have mine eyes out of their spheres been fitted.* 'How have mine eyes started from their hollows in the fever fits of my disease.' Dowden.

120. 9, 10. *O, that our night of woe might have re-member'd My deepest sense, how hard true sorrow hits.*
O, that the memory of our night of suffering might have recalled (remember'd) to my inmost soul how hard a blow true sorrow strikes.

121. 3, 4. *And the just pleasure lost, which is so deem'd Not by our feeling, but by others' seeing.* 'And the legitimate pleasure lost, which is deemed vile, not by us who experience it, but by others who look on and condemn.' Dowden. 'And the lawful pleasure lost, which is judged vile from the point of view of others and not from any sense of shame on our part.' Wyndham.

122. In this sonnet Shakespeare explains why he gave away a blank book, a present from his friend. Compare sonnet 77.

122. 10. *Nor need I tallies thy dear love to score.* This line alludes to the old custom of recording by cutting notches (scores) on a stick (tally).

123. 7, 8. *And rather make them born to our desire Than think that we before have heard them told.* 'We regard the wonderful works of to-day as the offspring of our own will, and forget that past ages produced the very same.' Beeching.

124. 4. *Weeds among weeds, or flowers with flowers gather'd.* Time might weed it out with hate or gather it lovingly as a flower.

124. 13, 14. *To this I witness call the fools of time, Which die for goodness, who have liv'd for crime.* Scholars are not agreed as to the meaning of this obscure couplet. 'The fools of time' may be Essex and his followers; the Jesuits, condemned for plotting against the Crown; or any traitors who die piously.

125. 13, 14. *Hence, thou suborn'd informer! a true soul When most impeach'd stands least in thy control.* In this sonnet Shakespeare has asserted that he regards not outward appearance but the heart. Probably there is no personal reference in 'suborn'd informer'; it means any false idea or detraction of the poet's devotion.

126.   The Quarto indicates by brackets that two lines are missing after the final couplet, yet this twelve-line poem, written not in sonnet form but in couplets, is complete as it stands.   It serves to mark the conclusion of the sonnets addressed to the friend.

127.   The dark woman of the following sonnets is as much a mystery as ever, despite the many pages that editors, critics, and playwrights have devoted to her.   Some scholars and dramatists assume her to be a maid of honor of Queen Elizabeth, Mary Fitton, at one time the mistress of William Herbert, Earl of Pembroke.   She was evidently attractive, for she was married twice after the Pembroke affair.   With the praise of dark beauty in this sonnet compare *Love's Labour's Lost* IV. iii. 247-265.

127. 1.   *In the old age black was not counted fair.* 'Black' in this sonnet and in the following ones, means 'dark complexioned,' 'brunette'; while 'fair' means both 'light complexioned' and 'beautiful.'

128. 5.   *jacks.* 'In the virginal, an upright piece of wood fixed to the key-lever and fitted with a quill which plucked the string as the jack rose when the key was pressed down. Here used as "key." ' Onions.

129. 1-3.   *The expense of spirit in a waste of shame Is lust in action; and till action, lust Is perjur'd.* Lust when put into action spends the spirit in a shameful waste; and until it acts, Lust is perjur'd.

135.   In this and in the following sonnet, Shakespeare writes a series of puns on the word 'will,' using it as a proper name, as 'wish,' and as 'lust.' Used as a proper name, *'Will* in over-plus; More than enough am I' (ll. 2, 3), refers to Shakespeare; *'Will* to boot,' (l. 2) refers to another man, possibly to the friend of sonnet 133, l. 2.

138. In *The Passionate Pilgrim*, 1599, this sonnet was printed with variations from the present text in eight of its lines. In general, the present version seems the better one and probably represents Shakespeare's revision of the poem published ten years before the collected sonnets appeared.

141. 9. *five wits.* Common sense, imagination, fancy, estimation, memory.

144. This sonnet appeared in *The Passionate Pilgrim*, 1599, with some unimportant changes in text. (Cf. note on sonnet 138.) Drayton's sonnet, 'An evil spirit, your beauty, haunts me still,' published also in 1599, has certain resemblances to this sonnet. That Drayton took a hint from Shakespeare seems more probable than that Shakespeare was indebted to Drayton.

145. This sonnet seems out of place in this series on the 'female evil.' It is written in octosyllabics; and it depicts a woman quite different from that mistress, 'black in deeds,' whose baneful influence upon the poet has been described in the preceding sonnets.

146. 1, 2. *Poor soul, the centre of my sinful earth, Fool'd by these rebel powers that thee array.* In the Quarto, the second line of this couplet is misprinted 'My sinful earth these rebel powers that thee array.' In place of 'My sinful earth,' repeated from the first line, many readings have been proposed, such as: 'Foil'd by'; 'Slave of'; 'Thrall to'; 'Starved by.' The reading of this text is as plausible as any other.

153, 154. These two sonnets are alternative versions of an epigram by Marianus, a Byzantine writer of about the fifth century A. D. There were sixteenth-century translations of this epigram both in Latin and in Italian; in Giles Fletcher's *Licia*, 1593, there is another very free adaptation of it.

APPENDIX A

History of the Sonnets

The first mention of Shakespeare's sonnets occurs in a little book by Francis Meres entitled *Palladis Tamia, Wit's Treasury,* published in 1598: 'the sweet, witty soul of Ovid lives in mellifluous and honey-tongued Shakespeare, witness his *Venus and Adonis,* his *Lucrece,* his sugared sonnets among his private friends.' 'Among his private friends' means not only that the sonnets were unpublished, but that they were composed for persons with whom he was in intimate relations. The obscurity of many of these poems certainly arises from the fact that they were written for friendly eyes; and accordingly they contain many allusions to persons and events which would be plain enough to Shakespeare's circle, but which would mean little or nothing to outsiders, even in the poet's day.

In *The Passionate Pilgrim,* 1599, were published the first two of Shakespeare's sonnets to appear in print. They were Nos. 138 and 144. Their text differs in several lines from that printed in the first edition of the whole sonnet collection. This first edition, which the present volume follows, was a quarto published by Thomas Thorpe in 1609. It contains a large number of obvious mistakes that ruin the sense; in several cases sonnets that plainly should follow each other are separated; and it is impossible to believe that Shakespeare prepared the text for publication.

This first quarto made no such impression as did Sidney's posthumous sonnet sequence, *Astrophel and Stella,* published in 1591, and it was not until 1640 that a second edition of Shakespeare's sonnets appeared. This was published by John Benson under the title 'Poems written by Wil. Shake-speare, Gent.';

yet it contained, as well, poems by Marlowe, Raleigh, Ben Jonson, Carew, Herrick, Milton, and others. The sonnets were not printed in the order in which they appeared in the quarto of 1609. In many cases they were run together as one continuous poem; and there were added to them, singly or in groups, seventy-four titles, some fairly appropriate, others quite unfitting, and nearly all commonplace. Seven sonnets, including No. 18, 'Shall I compare thee to a summer's day,' and the poem in couplets, No. 126, are omitted from this edition. Plainly it is much inferior to the quarto of 1609. In 1710 both the first and second editions were reprinted. Two editions in a century indicate a lack of interest in the sonnets, especially when their fate is contrasted with the numerous editions and great popularity of many of the plays.

There is further evidence in the manner in which the first editors of Shakespeare neglected these poems. To cite Lee, 'Neither Nicholas Rowe, nor Pope, nor Theobald, nor Hanmer, nor Warburton, nor Capell, nor Dr. Johnson included them in their respective collections of Shakespeare's plays. None of these editors, save Capell, showed any signs of acquaintance with them.' The first critical edition of the sonnets was Malone's, 1780, for which George Steevens supplied some material; and it is indicative of the general attitude towards the sonnets that Steevens himself, in 1793, wrote that 'The strongest act of Parliament that could be framed would fail to compel readers into their service.'

With the rise of the Romantic School, the sonnets found readers, students, and imitators. Wordsworth, Coleridge, and Keats directed attention to them and on the Continent, where also they had suffered neglect, they became a subject of study and criticism. At the present moment, no part of Shakespeare's work arouses more interest or a greater critical discussion, a discussion which unfortunately has arrived at no sure conclusions.

APPENDIX B

Problems of the Sonnets

The numerous problems presented by this sonnet collection may be grouped under three heads: historical, literary, and autobiographical.

The historical problems are the identification of the men and women of this series, or the events hinted at in such a sonnet as No. 107. Who was W. H.? Is he the same person as the 'beauteous and lovely youth' of the first sonnets? Who was the poet whom Shakespeare considered 'better' and 'worthier' than himself? Who was the dark woman? (Cf. notes on pp. 78-79, 85, 89.) These questions are perpetually discussed, but never conclusively answered.

The two chief literary problems are: when were these sonnets written and in what order should they be printed? Plainly, from Meres's mention of them in 1598, many of the sonnets were composed long before the appearance of the first quarto in 1609, and just as clearly, many of the sonnets were printed out of their natural order.

In regard to the first question, it has been shown that there are more striking parallels between the sonnets and the earlier plays—*Love's Labour's Lost, Two Gentlemen of Verona, Romeo and Juliet*—than with the later, though the mood of *Troilus and Cressida, Hamlet, Antony and Cleopatra,* is sometimes reflected in this collection. Internal evidence is always dangerous, yet the general impression the sonnets make on the reader by their resemblances to *Venus and Adonis* (1593) and *The Rape of Lucrece* (1594), and by their fluency, their enthusiasm for beauty, their excess of emotion over reflection is that as a whole they are the work of the young Shakespeare. They may be assigned roughly to the years 1593-1598, which would bring them within the period of the greatest vogue of the Elizabethan sonnet. This assumption does not preclude the possibility that some of the sonnets were written much later, even in the reign of James I. Here is one more unsolved problem.

The order of the sonnets is a fascinating study. It has sometimes been assumed that sonnets Nos. 1-125 are all written to or about a lovely youth. It is certain that No. 126, the lyric in couplets, marks a division in the series and that most of the sonnets placed after it concern themselves directly or indirectly with the dark woman; but it does not follow as a corollary that all the sonnets before No. 126 refer to a man. There is no reason to assume that the original publisher, Thorpe, was close enough to Shakespeare to understand fully the different MSS. out of which he may have combined the whole series. It is easy to see that many of the sonnets are printed in their proper sequence (Nos. 1-17, 40-42, 63-65, 78-86, for example), but on the other hand some sonnets are clearly out of their natural order (cf. Nos. 70, 77, 81). It is not at all certain that all of the sonnets before No. 126 must refer to the youth Shakespeare praised, though Thorpe may have thought so or wished the reader to think so. Benson, the publisher of the second edition, would have the reader believe, from the titles affixed to the sonnets in his edition, that nearly all these poems were written to a woman. In five cases when the text of the first edition showed that to be impossible, he altered it, changing 'him' to 'her' and 'friend' or 'boy' to 'love.' (Nos. 101, 104, 108.)

The most disputed problem of all is the autobiographical value of this sequence. Opinions on this matter range from Sir Sidney Lee's conclusion that the sonnets, for all their beauty, are imitative and conventional, to unsubstantiated theories by Frank Harris and Arthur Acheson of the intimate, personal confessions of these poems. Certainly Lee has no difficulty in proving that many of the sonnets are conventional in both theme and treatment. The debates of the eye and heart (Nos. 46, 47) are merely the 'quirks of blazoning pen.' Like the sonnets of Wordsworth and Keats, these poems differ greatly in their content and in their value; and certain quibbling, punning ones, written for the amusement of the moment, seem unworthy of their author. But there are many others which must strike the unprejudiced reader as 'such fair speech as soul to soul affordeth.' Surely in many sonnets we have glimpses of Shakespeare the man. We see a poet who was deeply sensitive to appreciation and friendship, who felt the inferiority of his social position and the discouragements of his art, and who ranged from dejection to exultation, from vulgar ribaldry and cynical indecency to the inspiration of devoted friendship. In part, the inconsistencies in the moods of the sonnets are the inconsistencies of life itself. Shakespeare may not have 'unlocked his heart' in these poems; but surely at times he left the door ajar.

APPENDIX C

THE SONNET AND ELIZABETHAN SONNETEERS

It was Petrarch (1304-1374) who made the sonnet the most popular form of the lyric during the fifteenth and sixteenth centuries. Though sonnets had been written before him, notably by Dante, the vogue of Petrarch, overshadowing that of all other lyric poets ancient and modern, was carried far beyond 'this side idolatry.' His themes were love and beauty, a hopeless love thwarted by destiny and death. His followers and imitators were legion. Vagany, in his compendious bibliography of sixteenth-century French and Italian sonneteers, does not include them all, for no man has ever read them all or could survive if he made the attempt.

Before the sonnet reached England, it came to France, where Ronsard and his contemporaries were deeply influenced by Italian poetry; and in Shakespeare's day it was largely through the French sonneteers that Petrarch affected English writers, though they made direct translations of Italian sonnets as well. The first English sonnets were written by Sir Thomas Wyatt (1503-1542) and Henry Howard, Earl of Surrey (1518-1547), and were first published after their death in *Tottel's Miscellany*, 1557. As might be presumed, both these poets were confirmed admirers of Petrarch, and their sonnets showed it.

The sonnet of Petrarch, commonly called the Italian sonnet, is a poem of fourteen lines divided into two parts of eight and six lines, the octave and the sestet. The octave was written abbaabba, while the sestet could have two or three rhymes, arranged in no fixed order save that the last two lines should not rhyme together. In the octave a thought, an emotion, a picture is completely presented and the verse sentence, so to speak, comes to an end. In the sestet, the explanation, the comment, the summing up of the whole matter is given. Wyatt attempted the Italian form, but found it too difficult to write correctly, and his sonnets end in rhymed couplets. Surrey, more of a stylist, devised a new and simpler form for the sonnet—three quatrains with a concluding couplet, and with no attempt to preserve the division of the octave and sestet. As a simple trial will prove, it is much harder to write a sonnet in the Italian form than to compose three quatrains and a couplet; and as the Elizabethans prized fluency, they preferred Surrey's form. In Shakespeare it reached its greatest beauty so that Surrey's form is now often called the 'Shakespearean' sonnet. It is interesting to notice that at times Shakespeare makes the break in the thought between the eighth and ninth lines that the Italian sonnet writers observed. This will be seen in 'When, in disgrace with fortune and men's eyes,' No. 29, or better still, in several sonnets printed together with the sestet beginning invariably with 'O,' Nos. 21-23, 71, 72, 76.

Apart from Shakespeare, the Elizabethan sonnet sequences most worthy of study are Sidney's *Astrophel and Stella,* 1591, Daniel's *Delia,* 1592, Drayton's *Idea,* 1594, and Spenser's *Amoretti,* 1595. To read them, or even their finest passages, but makes more apparent the supremacy of Shakespeare.

APPENDIX D

THE TEXT OF THE PRESENT EDITION

Although two of the sonnets in this collection, Nos. 138 and 144, were included in *The Passionate Pilgrim,* 1599, the first edition of the sonnets is the quarto which appeared in 1609 and which sold for five pence. This quarto was not sanctioned by Shakespeare; it is full of obvious errors and yet it is the accepted text. By permission, the text of this edition is that of Craig's Oxford Shakespeare, published by the Oxford Press, which follows the first quarto, correcting its mistakes.

In a few cases the editor has departed from Craig's
text, preferring the reading of the first quarto or some
generally accepted emendation. Minor changes of
spelling and punctuation are not recorded, but all
other variations from Craig's text are given below,
where Craig's readings are printed after the colon.

10. 1.	For shame deny Q: For shame! deny
16. 10.	Which this Time's pencil,: Which this, Time's pencil,
16. 13.	yourself, Q: yourself
26. 14.	Till then, Q: Till then
31. 1.	hearts: hearts, Q
59. 11.	Whether Q: Whe'r
66. 14.	Save that to die Q: Save that, to die
75. 9.	Sometime all Q: Sometime, all
84. 1.	most, Q: most?
84. 2.	you, Q: you?
84. 4.	grew?: grew.
84. 8.	story.: story,
85. 3.	Reserve Q: Deserve
88. 5.	weakness being Q: weakness, being
110. 9.	have Q: save
114. 3.	say Q: say,
141. 6.	feeling Q: feeling,

APPENDIX E

Suggestions for Collateral Reading

Raymond M. Alden: *The Sonnets of Shakespeare.*
From the Quarto of 1609 with variorum readings and
commentary. Philadelphia, 1914. (Indispensable for
a study of the sonnets.)

The following editions have valuable introductions
and notes:

Edward Dowden: *Sonnets of William Shakespeare.*
London, 1881.

Thomas Tyler: *Shakespeare's Sonnets*. London, 1890. (A presentation of the Herbert theory.)

George Wyndham: *Poems of Shakespeare*. London, 1898.

C. C. Stopes: *Shakespeare's Sonnets*. London, 1904. (The editor is an able defender of the Southampton theory. Cf. *The Life of Henry, Third Earl of Southampton, Shakespeare's Patron,* Cambridge, England, 1922, by the same writer.)

H. C. Beeching: *Sonnets of Shakespeare*. Boston, 1904.

Sidney Lee: *Shakespeare's Sonnets*. A reproduction in facsimile of the first edition (1609). Oxford, 1905.

Sidney Lee: *Elizabethan Sonnets, newly arranged and indexed*. London, 1904.

J. Vianey: *Le Pétrarquisme en France au XVIme siècle*. Montpellier, 1909.

William Sharp: *Sonnets of this Century*. London, N. D. (The introduction contains a valuable discussion of the sonnet form and its history.)

H. D. Gray: 'The Arrangement and Date of Shakespeare's Sonnets.' Publications of the Modern Language Association of America. Boston, 1915.

A. C. Bradley: 'Shakespeare the Man,' in *Oxford Lectures on Poetry*. London, 1909.

The characters of the sonnets in fiction:

Oscar Wilde: *The Portrait of Mr. W. H.* London, 1889; Bernard Shaw: *The Dark Lady of the Sonnets*. London, 1914; Clemence Dane: *Will Shakespeare*. London, 1921.

INDEX OF WORDS GLOSSED

(Figures in full-faced type refer to page-numbers)

abuse: **21** (42. 7)
accessary: **18** (35. 13)
acquaintance strangle: **45** (89. 8)
action: **33** (65. 4)
adder's sense: **56** (112. 10)
adjunct (adj.): **46** (91. 5)
adjunct (noun): **61** (122. 13)
advance: **39** (78. 13)
advantage: **77** (153. 2)
adventurer in setting forth: (Dedication 10-12)
advis'd respects: **25** (49. 4)
against: **19** (38. 6); **25** (49. 1); **32** (63. 1)
aggravate: **73** (146. 10)
all tyrant: **75** (149. 4)
allow: **56** (112. 4)
ambassage: **13** (26. 3)
amiss: **18** (35. 7)
antique: **10** (19. 10)
antique hours: **34** (68. 9)
antiquity: **31** (62. 10)
approve: **21** (42. 8); **35** (70. 5); **74** (147. 7)
argument: **19** (38. 3)
art: **7** (14. 10)
as: **31** (62. 8); **39** (78. 3)
astonished: **43** (86. 8)
at height: **8** (15. 7)
attaint: **41** (82. 2)
authorizing: **18** (35. 6)

badges of either's woe: **22** (44. 14)
bail: **67** (133. 10)
bastard signs of fair: **34** (68. 3)
beated and chopp'd: **31** (62. 10)

beauteous blessings: **42** (84. 13)
beauteous roof: **5** (10. 7)
becoming of: **64** (127. 13)
begetter: (Dedication 1)
being made: **25** (50. 8)
bestow'st: **6** (11. 3)
better equipage: **16** (32. 12)
better spirit: **40** (80. 2)
better'd that: **38** (75. 8)
bettering . . . time: **16** (32. 5)
bevel: **61** (121. 11)
black: **64** (127. 1)
blazon: **53** (106. 5)
blenches: **55** (110. 7)
blood: **55** (109. 10)
bore the canopy: **63** (125. 1)
born to our desire: **62** (123. 7)
both twain: **21** (42. 11)
both your poets: **42** (83. 14)
bounty: **27** (53. 11)
brand: **56** (111. 5); **77** (153. 1)
brass eternal slave: **32** (64. 4)
brave: **6** (12. 2)
bravery: **17** (34. 4)
buds of marjoram: **50** (99. 7)
but: **13** (25. 6); **66** (131. 10)
by art: **70** (139. 4)
by waning grown: **63** (126. 3)

came: **67** (134. 11)
canker: **48** (95. 2)
canker-blooms: **27** (54. 5)
captain: **26** (52. 8)
carcanet: **26** (52. 8)

cast his utmost sum: **25** (49. 3)

censures: **74** (148. 4)

character: **54** (108. 1)

charge: **73** (146. 8)

charg'd: **35** (70. 10)

charter of thy worth: **44** (87. 3)

check (verb): **68** (136. 1)

check (noun): **29** (58. 7)

cheer: **49** (97. 13)

cheered and check'd: **8** (15. 6)

chest: **26** (52. 9)

chief: **21** (42. 3)

child of state: **62** (124. 1)

clear: **42** (84. 10)

closure: **24** (48. 11)

come in the rearward: **45** (90. 6)

comment: **45** (89. 2)

common: **35** (69. 14)

compare: **65** (130. 14)

compile: **39** (78. 9)

composed wonder: **30** (59. 10)

compounded: **36** (71. 10)

conceit: **8** (15. 9); **54** (108. 13)

confin'd doom: **54** (107. 4)

confounds: **3** (5. 6); confounding: **32** (63. 10)

consum'd . . . nourish'd by: **37** (73. 12)

content: **1** (1. 11)

contracted: **1** (1. 5); **28** (56. 10)

converted: **4** (7. 11)

convertest: **6** (11. 4)

correct correction: **56** (111. 12)

countenance: **43** (86. 13)

counterfeit: **27** (53. 5)

counterpart: **42** (84. 11)

crooked: **30** (60. 7)

cross: **45** (90. 2)

curious: **19** (38. 13)

damask'd: **65** (130. 5)

darkly: **22** (43. 4)

date: **7** (14. 14)

dateless: **15** (30. 6); **77** (153. 6)

dates: **62** (123. 5)

dead seeing: **34** (67. 6)

dearest spite: **19** (37. 3)

debate: **45** (89. 13)

debateth: **8** (15. 11)

defeat: **31** (61. 11)

defeated: **10** (20. 11)

delves the parallels: **30** (60. 10)

departest: **6** (11. 2)

desire . . . shall neigh: **26** (51. 10, 11)

determinate: **44** (87. 4)

determination: **7** (13. 6)

dial-hand: **52** (104. 9)

difference: **53** (105. 8)

dignified: **51** (101. 4)

disabled: **33** (66. 8)

discloses: **27** (54. 8)

disgrace: **17** (33. 8)

disperse: **39** (78. 4)

distils: **27** (54. 14)

divining: **53** (106. 11)

do define: **31** (62. 7)

doth lie: **62** (123. 11)

doth part his function: **57** (113. 3)

double-vantage: **44** (88. 12)

doubting: **38** (75. 6)

dressings: **62** (123. 4)

drop in: **45** (90. 4)

eager compounds: **59** (118. 2)

edge of doom: **58** (116. 12)

effectually: **57** (113. 4)

eisel: **56** (111. 10)

endeared: **16** (31. 1)

ending doom: **28** (55. 12)

engraft you new: **8** (15. 14)

engrafted: **19** (37. 8)

engross'd: **67** (133. 6)

enlarg'd: **35** (70. 12)
enlighten: **76** (152. 11)
entertain: **20** (39. 11)
entitled: **19** (37. 7)
erst: **6** (12. 6)
esteeming: **51** (102. 3)
estimate: **44** (87. 2)
every one, one shade: **27** (53. 3)
exchang'd: **55** (109. 7)
excusing thy sins: **18** (35. 8)
expense: **15** (30.8)
expense of spirit: **65** (129. 1)
expiate: **11** (22. 4)
extreme: **65** (129. 4)

fair: **8** (16. 11); **64** (127. 1)
fairing . . . face: **64** (127. 6)
fairly: **3** (5. 4)
fame: **42** (84. 11)
fashion: **62** (124. 8)
favour: **57** (113. 10)
fear of trust: **12** (23. 5)
fee: **60** (120. 13)
fil'd: **43** (85. 4)
fire . . . out: **72** (144. 14)
five wits: **71** (141. 9)
fleets: **10** (19. 5)
foison: **27** (53. 9)
fond: **2** (3. 7)
fond on praise: **42** (84. 14)
fools of time: **62** (124. 13)
for: **20** (40. 6); **26** (52. 4); **50** (99. 6); **62** (124. 2)
for love: **26** (51. 12)
for store: **6** (11. 9)
forward: **50** (99. 1)
foul: **66** (132. 14)
fountains: **18** (35. 2)
frank: **2** (4. 4)
free: **2** (4. 4); **63** (125. 10)
frequent: **59** (117. 5)
fresh repair: **2** (3. 3)
from me: **72** (144. 11)
front: **51** (102. 7)

furthest earth remov'd: **22** (44. 6)
fury: **50** (100. 3)

gave . . . youth: **55** (110. 7)
gaze: **3** (5. 2)
give another place: **40** (79. 4)
give salutation to: **61** (121. 6)
give warning to the world: **36** (71. 3)
given to time: **59** (117. 6)
gives . . . place: **54** (108. 11)
go: **26** (51. 14)
gor'd: **55** (110. 3)
grievances foregone: **15** (30. 9)
grind: **55** (110. 10)
grossly: **50** (99. 5)
guilty goddess . . . deeds: **56** (111. 2)
gulls: **43** (86. 10)

had: **38** (75. 12)
haply: **45** (89. 12)
happies: **3** (6. 6)
have astronomy: **7** (14. 2)
have what . . . end: **55** (110. 9)
heart: **57** (113. 5)
heavy Saturn: **49** (98. 4)
height: **58** (116. 8)
highmost pitch: **4** (7. 9)
himself: **24** (47. 4)
his: **5** (9. 10)
hugely politic: **62** (124. 11)
humour: **46** (91. 5); **46** (92. 8)
husbandry: **7** (13. 10)

idle rank: **61** (122. 3)
if never intermix'd: **51** (101. 8)
ill-wresting: **70** (140. 11)
imaginary: **14** (27. 9)

impanelled: **23** (46. 9)
impression: **56** (112. 1)
imprison'd . . . liberty: **29** (58. 6)
in character: **30** (59. 8)
in love's fresh case: **54** (108. 9)
in manners: **43** (85. 1)
in my purpose bred: **56** (112. 13)
in proof: **65** (129. 11)
in the onset: **45** (90. 11)
in their gazing spent: **63** (125. 8)
in their wills: **61** (121. 8)
in this: **54** (107. 13)
in your report: **42** (83. 5)
inconstant stay: **8** (15. 9)
indigest: **57** (114. 5)
indirectly: **34** (67. 7)
influence: **39** (78. 10)
inhearse: **43** (86. 3)
intend: **14** (27. 6)
interest: **16** (31. 7); **37** (74. 3)
invention: **19** (38. 8)
is that: **37** (74. 13)
it: **57** (113. 5)
itself and true: **34** (68. 10)

jacks: **64** (128. 5)
just to the time: **55** (109. 7)

kept: **74** (147. 6)
kingly: **57** (114. 10)

labouring for invention: **30** (59. 3)
lace itself: **34** (67. 4)
latch: **57** (113. 6)
lay: **51** (101. 7)
leese: **3** (5. 14)
level: **59** (117. 11)
liberty: **21** (41. 1)
life's composition: **23** (45. 9)
like: **66** (132. 12)
like as: **59** (118. 1)

like none: **27** (53. 14)
lilies that fester: **47** (94. 14)
limbecks: **60** (119. 2)
limit: **41** (82. 6)
lines of life: **8** (16. 9)
liquid prisoner: **3** (5. 10)
livery: **1** (2. 3)
look strange: **45** (89. 8)
lovely argument: **40** (79. 5)

made more or less: **62** (123. 12)
main: **30** (60. 5)
makeless: **5** (9. 4)
making . . . compare: **11** (21. 5)
man in hue: **10** (20. 7)
map: **34** (68. 1)
mask'd not thy show: **35** (70. 13)
master: **53** (106. 8)
may stain: **17** (33. 14)
measure: **46** (91. 7)
mended: **30** (59. 11)
merchandiz'd: **51** (102. 3)
minion: **63** (126. 9)
misplac'd: **33** (66. 5)
misuse: **76** (152. 7)
Mr. W. H.: (Dedication 3)
modern: **42** (83. 7)
moiety: **23** (46. 12)
more and less: **48** (96. 3)
mortal: **54** (107. 5)
motley: **55** (110. 2)
muse: **11** (21. 1)
music to hear: **4** (8. 1)
mutual ordering: **4** (8. 10)
my love receivest: **20** (40. 5)
my name: **36** (72. 11)
my next self: **67** (133. 6)
myself bring . . . stain: **55** (109. 8)
my unkind abuse: **67** (134. 12)

needy nothing: **33** (66. 3)
new-fangled ill: **46** (91. 3)

new-fired: **77** (153. 9)
new pride: **38** (76. 1)
new wail: **15** (30. 4)
newer: **62** (123. 2)
no beauty lack: **64** (127. 11)
none you: **27** (53. 14)
nor he will not be free: **67** (134. 5)
nor Mars his: **28** (55. 7)
noted weed: **38** (76. 6)

obsequious: **16** (31. 5)
o'er-green: **56** (112. 4)
of settled gravity: **25** (49. 8)
of that: **37** (74. 13)
of thee: **37** (74. 12)
office: **51** (101. 13)
offices: **39** (77. 13)
oft predict: **7** (14. 8)
old excuse: **1** (2. 11)
one on another's neck: **66** (131. 11)
on proof . . . accumulate: **59** (117. 10)
only is their show: **27** (54. 9)
or: **38** (75. 14)
or all away: **38** (75. 14)
or whether doth: **57** (114. 1)
ornament: **35** (70. 3)
other: **31** (62. 8)
other mine: **67** (134. 3)
out of their spheres . . . fitted: **60** (119. 7)
outward walls: **73** (146. 4)
owe: **35** (70. 14)
ow'st: **9** (18. 10)

pain: **19** (38. 14); **71** (141. 14)
painted counterfeit: **8** (16. 8)
palate urge: **59** (118. 2)
parts of me: **16** (31. 11)
pass: **52** (103. 11)
past: **65** (129. 6)
patent: **44** (87. 8)
peace of you: **38** (75. 3)

perspective: **12** (24. 4)
Philomel: **51** (102. 7)
physic did except: **74** (147. 8)
pity-wanting pain: **70** (140. 4)
pointing: **7** (14. 6)
points: **13** (26. 10)
policy: **62** (124. 9)
poor retention: **61** (122. 9)
precious: **43** (85. 4)
preposterously: **55** (109. 11)
presage: **54** (107. 6)
presagers: **12** (23. 10)
presume not: **11** (22. 13)
prevent'st: **50** (100. 14)
pride: **26** (52. 12)
prime: **35** (70. 8)
privilege (noun): **48** (95. 13)
privilege (verb): **29** (58. 10)
process: **52** (104. 6)
proposed: **65** (129. 12)
proud-pied: **49** (98. 2)
prove: **36** (72. 4)
put besides: **12** (23. 2)

qualify **55** (109. 2)
quest: **23** (46. 10)
question make: **6** (12. 9)
quietus: **63** (126. 12)

rack: **17** (33. 6)
rage: **9** (17. 11)
ragged: **3** (6. 1)
rank: **43** (85. 12)
rank of: **59** (118. 12)
raz'd: **61** (122. 7)
receipt: **68** (136. 7)
reckoning: **58** (115. 5)
record: **30** (59. 5)
recur'd: **23** (45. 9)
refigur'd: **3** (6. 10)
region: **17** (33. 12)
register: **54** (108. 3)
rehearse: **11** (21. 4); **19** (38. 4); **36** (71. 11)
religious: **16** (31. 6)

remember'd: 60 (120. 9)
remember'd not to be: 2 (3. 13)
remove: 58 (116. 4)
remover: 58 (116. 4)
render: 63 (125. 12)
reserve: 16 (32. 7)
reserve their character: 43 (85. 3)
respect (noun): 18 (36. 5)
respect (verb): 43 (85. 13); 75 (149. 9)
resty: 50 (100. 9)
reviewest: 37 (74. 5)
rich-proud: 32 (64. 2)
richly compil'd: 43 (85. 2)
right of sepulchres: 34 (68. 6)
rondure: 11 (21. 8)
rotten smoke: 17 (34. 4)
ruth: 66 (132. 4)

satire to decay: 50 (100. 11)
savour: 63 (125. 7)
scanted: 59 (117. 1)
scope: 15 (29. 7)
scope and tenour: 31 (61. 8)
seconds: 63 (125. 11)
seeming: 51 (102. 1)
seldom: 26 (52. 4)
self-doing: 29 (58. 12)
sense: 18 (35. 9)
separable: 18 (36. 6)
sequent toil: 30 (60. 4)
sessions: 15 (30. 1)
set a form: 45 (89. 6)
set me light: 44 (88. 1)
several: 69 (137. 9)
shadow: 19 (37. 10); 22 (43. 5)
shady stealth: 39 (77. 7)
shake hands: 14 (28. 6)
should you: 36 (72. 14)
show: 47 (94. 2); 53 (105. 2)
sickle hour: 63 (126. 2)
simplicity: 33 (66. 11)
simply: 69 (138. 7)

since: 33 (65. 1)
sit: 52 (103. 13)
slow offence: 26 (51. 1)
so: 64 (127. 13); 58 (115. 13)
so as: 66 (131. 1)
so thy praise: 35 (70. 11)
soil: 35 (69. 14)
solemn: 26 (52. 5)
sometime: 32 (64. 3)
sourly: 18 (35. 14)
sovereign eye: 17 (33. 2)
speaking in effect: 43 (85. 14)
spites: 20 (40. 14)
spoil: 33 (65. 12)
sportive: 61 (121. 6)
stain: 18 (35. 3)
staineth: 17 (33. 14)
state: 32 (64. 9, 10); 48 (96. 12)
statute of thy beauty: 67 (134. 9)
steel'd sense: 56 (112. 8)
steepy: 32 (63. 5)
stell'd: 12 (24. 1)
still: 5 (9. 5)
store . . . convert: 7 (14. 12)
stores: 34 (67. 13)
strained: 41 (82. 10)
strains: 45 (90. 13)
strangely: 25 (49. 5)
stretched: 9 (17. 12)
subdu'd: 56 (111. 6)
suborn'd informer: 63 (125. 13)
subscribes: 54 (107. 10)
successive: 64 (127. 3)
sufferance: 29 (58. 7)
suffic'd: 19 (37. 11)
suggest: 72 (144. 2)
suit: 66 (132. 12)
suited: 64 (127. 10)
summer's story: 49 (98. 7)
suppose: 29 (57. 10)
surety-like: 67 (134. 7)

suspect: **35** (70. 3)
sweet season'd: **38** (75. 2)
swerving: **44** (87. 8)
swift extremity: **26** (51. 6)
sympathiz'd: **41** (82. 11)

T. T.: (Dedication 13)
table: **12** (24. 2)
tables: **61** (122. 1, 12)
task: **36** (72. 1)
tell: **7** (14. 5); **15** (30. 10)
tender: **42** (83. 4)
terms: **73** (146. 11)
that: **27** (54. 14); **28** (55. 13); **55** (109. 5)
that able spirit: **43** (85. 7)
that is this: **37** (74. 14)
that more . . . expressed: **12** (23. 12)
that which I bring forth: **36** (72. 13)
the rest: **58** (115. 12)
then tender'd: **60** (120. 11)
thinly: **26** (52. 7)
this: **77** (154. 13)
thou single: **4** (8. 14)
though: **32** (63. 12)
though words . . . before: **43** (85. 12)
thought kills me: **22** (44. 9)
thralled discontent: **62** (124. 7)
thyself outgoing . . . noon: **4** (7. 13)
time remov'd: **49** (97. 5)
time-bettering days: **41** (82. 8)
times in hope: **30** (60. 13)
tincture: **27** (54. 6)
tires: **27** (53. 8)
to all the world: **41** (81. 6)
to be: **41** (81. 11)
to die: **33** (66. 14)
to each: **72** (144. 11)
to give away yourself: **8** (16. 13)

to give full growth: **58** (115. 14)
to linger out: **45** (90. 8)
to take a new acquaintance: **39** (77. 12)
to themselves: **27** (54. 11)
to tie up: **35** (70. 12)
to use: **67** (134. 10)
to weigh: **60** (120. 8)
torn: **76** (152. 3)
tract: **4** (7. 12)
transfix the flourish: **30** (60. 9)
translated: **48** (96. 8)
treasure: **3** (6. 3)
trim: **49** (98. 2)
trimm'd in jollity: **33** (66. 3)
twire: **14** (28. 12)

under thee: **39** (78. 4)
unear'd: **2** (3. 5)
unfair: **3** (5. 4)
unhappily forsworn: **33** (66. 4)
unjust: **69** (138. 9)
unknown: **59** (117. 5)
unlook'd for: **13** (25. 4)
unrespected: **22** (43. 2); **27** (54. 10)
unset: **8** (16. 6)
unsway'd: **71** (141. 11)
unthrifts: **7** (13. 13)
untold: **68** (136. 9)
untrimm'd: **9** (18. 8)
untrue (adj.): **57** (113. 14)
untrue (adv.): **36** (72. 10)
upon desired change: **45** (89. 6)
upon misprision growing: **44** (87. 11)
upon thy part: **44** (88. 6)
uprear: **25** (49. 11)
use: **3** (6. 5); **39** (78. 3)

vade: **27** (54. 14)
varying to other words: **53** (105. 10)

vaunt: **8** (15. 7)

wards of trust: **24** (48. 4)
warrantise: **75** (150. 7)
was consecrate: **37** (74. 6)
waste blanks: **39** (77. 10)
watching: **74** (148. 10)
wear . . . out of memory: **8** (15. 8)
wear this world out: **28** (55. 12)
weed: **1** (2. 4)
weeds among weeds: **62** (124. 4)
welfare: **59** (118. 7)
well-contented day: **16** (32. 1)
were't: **63** (125. 1)
what . . . 'greeing: **57** (114. 11)
what thou dost hide: **71** (142. 13)
when as: **25** (49. 3)
whe'r: **30** (59. 11)
where: **22** (44. 4)
whereto: **62** (124. 8)
whether revolution be the same: **30** (59. 12)
which: **32** (64. 13); **37** (74. 4)
which physic did except: **74** (147. 8)
whose shadow . . . bright: **22** (43. 5)

wilfully: **40** (80. 8)
Will: **68** (135. 1); **72** (143. 13)
wink: **22** (43. 1)
wiry concord: **64** (128. 4)
with compare: **18** (35. 6)
with infection: **34** (67. 1)
with manners: **20** (39. 1)
with my extern: **63** (125. 2)
with my neglect . . . dispense: **56** (112. 12)
with thee partake: **75** (149. 2)
wits: **71** (141. 9)
wonder at: **49** (98. 9)
woo'd of time: **35** (70. 6)
words come hindmost: **43** (85. 12)
world's due: **1** (1. 14)
world-without-end: **29** (57. 5)
worse essays: **55** (110. 8)
worth: **58** (116. 8)
would be: **36** (71. 7)
wrack: **63** (126. 5)
wrack'd: **40** (80. 11)
wrackful: **33** (65. 6)
wretched minutes kill: **63** (126. 8)
wrought: **22** (44. 11)

youngly: **6** (11. 3)
yourself: **7** (13. 1)